Gender-Based Violence and Digital Media in South Africa

This book presents a new paradigm for attending to gender-based violence (GBV) social media discourse among marginalised Black women in South Africa.

Focusing on the intersections of television and social media, the study charts the morphing and merging of the "inside" of the soap opera and the "outside" of the real world, amid a rise in feminist social media activism. The analysis begins with coverage of gender-based violence in a long-running South African soap opera and social media discussion of these issues, in parallel with real-world events and the collective social media response. The author offers pertinent insights into audiences in sub-Saharan Africa, presenting a new feminist trajectory for women and activism in the region.

Offering new insights into an important issue, this book will be of interest to scholars and students of gender, cultural studies, film studies, television studies, sociology, development studies, feminism, media, and journalism.

Millie Mayiziveyi Phiri was a University of Johannesburg postdoctoral fellow during 2020–2021 and specialises in research in digital technologies, freedom of expression, gender, and health research. An award-winning journalist with extensive experience working in Africa, she spearheaded the setting up of the first of its kind, Graca Machel Trust Pan African Network of Women Journalists.

Routledge Focus on Media and Cultural Studies

Community Media and Identity in Ireland
Jack Rosenberry

Cultural Chauvinism
Intercultural Communication and the Politics of Superiority
Minabere Ibelema

Crowdfunding and Independence in Film and Music
Blanka Brzozowska and Patryk Galuszka

Building Communities of Trust
Creative Work for Social Change
Ann E. Feldman

Secrecy in Public Relations, Mediation and News Cultures
The Shadow World of the Media Sphere
Anne Cronin

Spanish Horror Film and Television in the 21st Century
Vicente Rodríguez Ortega and Rubén Romero Santos

Gender-Based Violence and Digital Media in South Africa
Millie Phiri

Gender-Based Violence and Digital Media in South Africa

By
Millie Mayiziveyi Phiri

LONDON AND NEW YORK

First published 2024
by Routledge
4 Park Square, Milton Park, Abingdon, Oxon OX14 4RN

and by Routledge
605 Third Avenue, New York, NY 10158

Routledge is an imprint of the Taylor & Francis Group, an informa business

© 2024 Millie Mayiziveyi Phiri

The right of Millie Mayiziveyi Phiri to be identified as author of this work has been asserted in accordance with sections 77 and 78 of the Copyright, Designs and Patents Act 1988.

All rights reserved. No part of this book may be reprinted or reproduced or utilised in any form or by any electronic, mechanical, or other means, now known or hereafter invented, including photocopying and recording, or in any information storage or retrieval system, without permission in writing from the publishers.

Trademark notice: Product or corporate names may be trademarks or registered trademarks, and are used only for identification and explanation without intent to infringe.

British Library Cataloguing-in-Publication Data
A catalogue record for this book is available from the British Library

ISBN: 978-1-032-18688-7 (hbk)
ISBN: 978-1-032-19781-4 (pbk)
ISBN: 978-1-003-26082-0 (ebk)

DOI: 10.4324/9781003260820

Typeset in Times New Roman
by Deanta Global Publishing Services, Chennai, India

To God be the glory

Contents

List of figures ix
Acknowledgements x
Acronyms xi

1 Is digital feminist activism defining GBV? 1
Introduction 1
Violence against women in South Africa 2
Scandal! *characters 7*
The manufacture of female fear 18
Book structure 22
Limitations 23
Notes 25
References 26

2 Gender-based violence and digital technologies 30
Introduction 30
Sociality of social media: a discussion of Facebook and Twitter 30
Role of small screens 35
Soap opera fantasy or reality? 37
Notes 40
References 40

3 African feminist ideology politics and gender-based violence 43
Introduction 43
What's GBV got to do with representation and online identity? 46
Which feminism? 50
Notes 66
References 66

4 Gender digital activism offline and online GBV "talk" 71
Introduction 71
Is #AmINext a rhetoric or real question? 75
Clicktivism: social resistance or waste of time? 79
Where next for social media activism? 81
Note 82
References 82

5 The nature of GBV social media "talk," language, audiences 85
Introduction 85
Misogyny or blind male machismo and masculine virility? 95
Power of social media feminist activism 101
Social media "talk" and freedom of expression 109
Notes 111
References 112

Epilogue 115

Index 119

Figures

1.1	Obakeng slaps Gloria	13
1.2	Gloria's bruised and battered face	14
1.3	Gloria and Obakeng's "special" wedding	15
2.1	etvScandal Facebook followers	33
5.1	The frequency of mentioning the words "men" and "women"	91
5.2	Participants did not hold back in their views	102

Acknowledgements

Many thanks to friends, academic colleagues, and family, too numerous to mention here. This book would not have been possible without your many contributions and ideas. Special thanks to Kashan Krawitz for helping me with artistic work. To my four girls, Kundai Michelle, Tinotenda Lois, Nkensane Alfreda, and Mandidaishe Olyn – I am grateful for your understanding, patience, and encouragement as I authored this book.

Acronyms

etv	e-television
FOMO	fear of missing out
GBV	gender-based-violence
HIV	human immunodeficiency virus
IPV	intimate partner violence
PTSD	post-traumatic stress disorder
SADC	Southern Africa Development Community
UN	United Nations
VAW	violence against women
WEF	World Economic Forum
WHO	World Health Organisation

1 Is digital feminist activism defining GBV?

Introduction

This book is about digital media feminist activism and the role it plays to help us understand new knowledge about gender-based violence (GBV) that is targeted at Black marginalised women in South Africa. It is based on the analysis of 2015 episodes of one of South Africa's longest-running soap operas, *Scandal!*, regarding GBV, and South Africa's 2019 hashtag, #AmINext, sparked after a female student in Cape Town, South Africa, was murdered in a post office. *Scandal!* and #AmINext are both examples of how the intersection between new media, such as social television and small screens, plays a role in triggering and spreading "talk" and helps us to see GBV in new light. This book is hence a critical analysis of the digital media feminist activism against gender violence at a time when the GBV and Femicide National Strategic Plan Steering Committee in South Africa, in its 2020 report, described the country as the most unsafe place to be for a woman. In the report, the committee warns about how gender violence in the country has become "hyperendemic" (National strategic plan on gender-based violence & femicide report 2020). Later, this book sets up questions about the potential role of media, such as television, to promote specific kinds of social change. In sum, the book is a multi-perspective exploration that brings key concepts of "talk," social media/Facebook, soap opera/audience, and gender-based-violence into the spotlight.

When local soap opera *Scandal!* – a Monday-to-Friday drama set in a newsroom, centring on the interlaced personal lives of the staff who work in that newsroom – ran episodes on violence against women at the end of 2014 and beginning of 2015, viewers took to the soap opera's Facebook page to comment about the representation. This is what inspired the writing of this book. The comments related to six purposively sampled episodes of violence perpetrated against a female character, Gloria, by her second husband, Obakeng. *Scandal!* was an important source of study because it is one of the longest-running television dramas in South Africa, having been shown since 2005. It is viewed by 5 million South Africans on prime-time television, making it one of the most viewed shows in the country (Gaines, 2015). The show's plot outline is based on pressured "professional and personal lives of management and journalists" colliding "as they rush to find exclusives, meet

2 Is digital feminist activism defining GBV?

deadlines, push to make the big bucks and increase sales." Spence (2001, p. 183) alludes to the fact that relating soap operas to "real" people in a "knowable landscape" appeals to viewers who enjoy watching people and places that they are familiar with, giving texts a "real life" effect. This point is true, as we will learn later in the book how digital media audiences treated Gloria's abuse by Obakeng as real, offering solutions and relating it to their own lived experiences.

Data from the "Friends" of the "etvScandal" Facebook page who liked and posted comments, pictures, and videos relating to these episodes is analysed in this book to help us understand this digital media feminist activism trend aimed at making sense of GBV. The book also intermittently utilises the analysis of the 2019 Twitter hashtag #AmINext that trended after a Cape Town University student, Uyinene Mrwetyana, was murdered at a post office where she had gone to collect a parcel. Her death was followed by numerous other murders of women in South Africa, with women using the hashtag in a way that gives us a peek into the GBV that affects ordinary and marginalised Black women. This kind of GBV is hardly covered by the mainstream media, and the patterns remain unknown. Despite the fact that *Scandal!* was fictional and Twitter's #AmINext involved murders of real South African women, the audience's reactions to GBV on both social media platforms reveal how boundaries about online and offline lives have become blurred.

But what makes GBV so pervasive in South Africa? The next section tackles that question.

Violence against women in South Africa

In South Africa, GBV is an umbrella term used to capture violence that occurs because of the unequal power relations and the normative role expectations associated with each gender in any given society (Izumi, 2007, p. 14). Murders of women and children in the country – including femicide, also known as intimate partner violence (IPV) – are classified as GBV, although terms like domestic violence and violence against women (VAW) are also used to refer to murders of women, so this book will use them interchangeably. *Scandal!'s* case study, which this book is based on, devotes more attention to IPV. The #AmINext hashtag which this book is also premised on is a mixture of IPV and murders of women by men who are not necessarily their spouses. Abrahams et al. (2012), have simply defined intimate femicide or intimate partner femicide as the "killing of women by intimate partners (i.e., a current or former husband/boyfriend, same-sex partner, or rejected would-be lover)."

Physical abuse is defined as slapping, punching, kicking, pushing, grabbing, shoving, pulling out hair, and hitting (Mega et al., 2000).[1] Serious forms include burning, shooting, stabbing, beating with objects such as a hammer, baseball bat, or a belt causing deaths, deformities, disfigurements, internal injuries, harm to an unborn baby, broken teeth, and other serious body injuries. The United Nations Declaration on the Elimination of Violence against Women defines the term violence against women in Article 1 as:

> Any act of gender-based-violence that results in, or is likely to result in, physical, sexual or psychological harm or suffering to women, including threats of such acts, coercion or arbitrary deprivations of liberty, whether occurring in public or in private life.

Physical abuse itself has both physical and psychological dimensions. Izumi (2007, p. 14) notes that psychosocial damage and the threat of further violence contribute to the erosion of a woman's self-esteem, inhibiting her ability to defend herself or act against her abuser. This psychosocial effect of gender violence against women tends to be more systemic and subtler. And because these effects are harder to notice, they are also harder to diagnose and treat. On *Scandal!*, we saw that Obakeng's brand of violence did not just assume a single form, but was complex. This book is thus interested in seeing the extent to which audiences talking on social media identified these complexities.

The book draws on the UN's definition of GBV extensively, while also modifying it where necessary. The importance of this definition for this book is that it draws attention to gender violence within both the private and public spaces. The "talk" about gender violence on social media tended to draw on notions of violence in the context of private and public spheres. The representation of violence on *Scandal!* also tended to cross and intersperse the public and the private.

The UN has further expanded the definition of gender-based violence to refer to violations of the rights of women in situations of armed conflict, including systematic rape, sexual slavery, and forced pregnancy; forced sterilisation, forced abortion, coerced or forced use of contraceptives; prenatal sex selection and female infanticide, although the book does not touch on these. The UN further recognises the vulnerabilities of women from minority backgrounds, the elderly and the displaced, the indigenous, refugees, and migrant communities, the disabled, and women living in impoverished rural or remote areas, or in detention.

Although books like this one are key in showing us contemporary feminist audience responses to GBV using new media platforms, it is important to note that the *initial* impetus for the recognition of domestic violence as a social problem appears to have started in the 1970s through the efforts of the global women's and feminist movement (Joachim, 2007, p. 122; Antrobus, 2004, p. 29). As a research problem, it was not until the middle of the 20th century that serious and systematic academic inquiries commenced (Kurst-Swanger and Petcosky, 2003, p. 27). The studies presented at the 1993 meeting offered, for the first time, systematic evidence that violence against women was an international, underreported, and *structural* problem caused by the vulnerable, precarious, and low status of most women, particularly in the developing world. At the same time, efforts to recognise GBV as a human rights issue were aided by feminist action such as that taken by the likes of Carrillo (1991, p. 42), who was able to frame violence against women as a development issue in the 1990s, arguing that "gender violence interferes with women's own personal development by limiting their ability to pursue options in almost every area including the home, schools, workplaces, and most public spaces." For instance, the 1993 meeting succeeded in placing VAW on the agenda of the Human Rights Conference for the first time (Antrobus, 2004, p. 94). It culminated in the United Nations' adoption of the Declaration on the Elimination of All Forms of Violence against Women, a declaration that condemned, and drew attention to gender violence within both the private and the public spheres (Joachim, 2007, p. 1). Specifically, violence against women was categorised as a violation of human rights, identified as a universal problem, and duly criminalised. Before then, violence against women and reproductive rights and health were treated as domestic and private. The linkage of women's rights and human rights was a powerful frame for mobilising an international constituency against a structural and systemic problem. It was successful in that it resonated with women in different cultural contexts (Joachim, 2007, p. 124).

Violence against women in South Africa cuts across all races, classes, socio-economic standings, and educational backgrounds, although vulnerable marginalised women are more at risk than other women because they cannot afford to protect themselves – as we will discuss later, that even the laws are not enough. The effect of domestic violence on nations, communities, and families, though difficult to quantify *precisely*, is regarded as enormous (Kurst-Swanger and Petcosky, 2003, p. 8). Globally, at least one in every three women has been beaten, coerced into sex, or otherwise abused by an intimate partner in her lifetime (Joachim, 2007, p. 103). Such statistics played a role in South Africa holding its first National Conference on Violence against Women in Cape Town in 1995. Gender violence statistics in South Africa indicated that one in six women who die is killed by an intimate partner (Pillay, 2010, p. 68). These figures are higher in the poorest areas of South Africa, where one in three women reports physical violence, which is why this book significantly focuses on marginalised women and the impact of gender-based digital feminism activism. These figures could be higher if we take into account that most cases go unreported. Pillay (2010, p. 67) describes violence against women as the "biggest oppression" facing most South African women. This is truer if one defines violence in its systemic aspects that include poverty, lack of education, and lack of access to health, housing, and other necessities.

Data from across the world has indicated that *the home*, because of its privacy, has been by far the most dangerous place for women and frequently the site of cruelty, trauma, and torture (Joachim, 2007, p. 104). Fifty per cent of women in Tanzania, Ethiopia, Bangladesh, and Peru, for instance, had been subjected to violence because it happened in the privacy of homes. However, digital media feminist activism has critically changed how we perceive GBV as it is exposing what happens behind closed doors, such as in the home, into the open. The public/private dichotomy masks many forms of gender-based violence, particularly such acts as rape, incest, sexual assault, and domestic violence (Wies and Haldane, 2011, p. 3). Pillay (2010, p. 66) also observed that medical personnel did not investigate and report cases of violence against women unless the woman asked for help and reported the perpetrator. There is a fear that if women are required to report cases of violence against them, it will deter many women from seeking medical attention (Pillay, 2010, p. 66). Furthermore, cultural barriers exist that prevent women from reporting and talking about violence against them (Sibanda-Moyo et al., 2017, p. 47). This book supports the view that exposing the hidden sites of violence allows us to reflect on the structural factors that produce, reproduce, and exacerbate the suffering of the victim, and far too often protect the perpetrator. The book will help us to see how people talk about this form of pervasive but hard-to-report violence on social media, to shed light on the relationship between the reality of gender violence and the discourse of gender violence.

The feminist movement of the 1990s against GBV has influenced digital media feminist activism. Feminism will be analysed in detail in Chapter 3. Feminism, historically, has not been consistent nor homogeneous, as we will discuss later. It is this constant interference with a woman's full humanity that the book found to be salient about Obakeng's brand of violence in the six *Scandal!* episodes analysed. The aspects of gender violence explored in the book show that it is both complex and serious, and merits systematic study and documentation. This is because, as Carrillo (1991, p. 42) argues, gender violence "prevents women from contributing effectively to the economic development of a country because of its severe health and psychological impact," and we see this relating to Gloria.

Digital media feminist activism is new and has been on the rise in South Africa since 2017, with femicide-spawned controversial responses such as the hashtag #MenAreTrash, which was pointing out that women, like men, deserve to live in a free world, yet this is not so in South Africa, where women live in fear of being murdered. Despite its "epidemic" status in South Africa, however, violence against women is typically underreported, particularly in mainstream media.[2] This is even though it accounts for more than 50 per cent of all murders of women in South Africa (Willis, 2017). Willis claims less than 20 per cent of all femicides in South Africa are reported in the South African press annually. When femicides are eventually reported and mainstreamed in media discourse, it is often the case that they involve high-profile women, as happened in the case of the death of Reeva Steenkamp, a top South African model who was killed by her boyfriend, former South Africa Paralympics Oscar Pistorius, on Valentine's Day in 2013 (Willis, 2017), or because they have become some convenient *cause celebre*, as happened in the case of 22-year-old Karabo Mokoena, murdered in 2017. Mokoena's murder orchestrated a different kind of activism against GBV on digital media in South Africa. However, the GBV epidemic seems to have begun to peak around 2013, with the murder of Anene Booysen by her boyfriend. By 2019, when the Twitter hashtag #AmINext trended after a Cape Town University student Uyinene Mrwetyana was murdered at a post office where she had gone to collect a parcel, digital media feminist activism had caught on globally. The murders of Ntombizodwa Dlamini, Zolile Khumalo, Amanda Tweyi, Jabulile Nhlapo, and Siam Lee also made headlines[3] after Uyinene's murder. What these statistics, definitions, headlines, and hashtags reveal and reflect in the main is that violence against women takes specific forms, but also that such violence can be safely described as endemic (Sibanda-Moyo et al., 2017, p. 12; Mogale, Barns, and Richter, 2012). Hence, violence targeted at women on the margins is the central focus of this book, because of its topicality in contemporary South Africa and, secondly, because of the varied political, social, religious, and cultural perspectives – even controversies – it generates.

The GBV crisis is discussed in this book at a time when gender has become an important contemporary social change theme which has not been afforded adequate attention from communication studies perspectives. According to *Scandal!'s* head writer Grace Mahlaba (2023), it was the first time that *Scandal!* was telling the GBV story as it had become important that time, with a number of women being murdered in the country. The high incidences of GBV were happening despite the availability of international instruments that South Africa has signed such as Article 3 of the Universal Declaration of Human Rights (1948), which states that "Everyone has the right to life, liberty and security of person." Article 5 also reads: "No one shall be subjected to torture or to cruel, inhuman or degrading treatment or punishment" (Izumi, 2007, p. 14; Joachim, 2007, p. 5). Scholars of violence such as Zizek (2007) show that violence within a neoliberal order is generalised to the whole society. That violence will affect you, whether you are a man or a woman. Some men face violence at the hands of other men, while others face violence at the hands of women (Izumi, 2007, p. 15). These kinds of gendered violence are worth studying too. What is unique about this book, which is different from others, is its examination of GBV conversations on assorted forms of digital media such as social television (soap opera) and social media (Facebook and Twitter) using smart devices (laptops, phones, tablets). The conversations are important because they are viewed from a feminist lens to deliberately bring out how women are central to this topical issue. Using a feminist lens does not mean that men are not affected, but makes the point that GBV affects more women than men, and in different ways. Ultimately, the problem not only impacts individuals, but is a societal challenge that affects the development growth of a country. Digital media feminist activism becomes part of the solution worthy of our attention. Analysing and documenting lessons of digital feminism activism is rare and yet critical to changing mindsets, behaviour, and attitudes to GBV.

Digital media feminism is thus a new form of understanding GBV with the perception that it is patriarchal. Specific provisions have been made in the Universal Declaration of Human Rights and the Convention on the Elimination of All Forms of Discrimination Against Women, which defines what constitutes discrimination against women and sets out an agenda to prevent, eradicate, and punish violence against women and girls (Ennaji and Sadiqi, 2011). Countries that have ratified or acceded to the Convention are legally bound to put its provisions into practice. They commit to submitting national reports on measures they have taken to comply with their treaty obligations. South Africa is a signatory to these statutory instruments (Sibanda-Moyo et al., 2017, p. 20).

Since violence is a learned behaviour (Rushton, 1982), media, including digital media, can play a role in helping to change it. South African television has traditionally relied on edutainment models to create awareness (Burton, 2012). Dramas and soap opera have functioned as behavioural change agents (Spence, 2001; p. 188). What is not yet fully known or appreciated, however, is the role of social media and its intersection with social television. This book is an attempt to unravel audiences' reaction to GBV on these digital platforms. This is fundamentally important because domestic violence is part of the structural violence within the context of hierarchical power arrangements that deny women the tools for self-development. High rates of battering are associated with decision making and economic arrangements that foster hierarchical nonparticipation, severely restrict access to collective resources, and de-emphasise collective accomplishment and responsibility (Tifft, 1993, p. 13). Knowing the views of people about GBV and how it affects them in digital media spaces is opening a new way of understanding gender violence. To help us conceptualise the ideas of this book, the next section offers an overview of *Scandal!* characters.

Scandal! characters

The Gloria/Obakeng domestic violence storyline coincided with the 16 Days of Activism, an internationally recognised event aimed at eradicating violence against women. According to head writer Grace Mahlaba, *Scandal!* is issue-driven. The 16 Days of Activism was the most appropriate time to tell the GBV story. The 16 days are marked from November 25 to December 10 of each year as extensions of the UN International Day for the Elimination of Violence against Women (Smith, 2005). The date was chosen after three sisters – Patricia, Minerva, and Maria Teresa – were brutally beaten and strangled to death on November 25, 1960, in the Dominican Republic.[4] The women were on their way to visit their husbands, who had been imprisoned for their participation in a resistance movement. The 16 days also include World AIDS

8 Is digital feminist activism defining GBV?

Day on December 1, as well as December 6 to commemorate the anniversary of the Montreal Massacre, when a man gunned down 14 engineering students for "being feminists." Antrobus (2004, p. 94) explains that the 16 Days of Activism "establishes a context in which women can express zero tolerance for violence." In some countries, such activism has been successfully used to get governments to pay attention to violations of women's human rights and take action to protect women.

Campaigns are thus increasingly being seen as the most effective way of breaking the silence that often shrouds the subject of violence against women, to raise awareness and help to change attitudes, policies, and practices. South Africa first adopted the 16 days campaign in 1998 as one of the intervention strategies towards creating a society free of violence. In 2014, the country decided that activism against violence on women should not just be confined to the 16 days. As such, the government adopted the campaign "365 Days for No Violence Against Women and Children" and the hashtag #CountMeIn. South Africa also recognises August of each year as Women's Month. But these campaigns have increasingly turned to digital spaces, which is why this book is about how television audiences "talked, commented about, and discussed specific social issues on social media, in this case, the representation of violence against women, with the intention of proposing a new interpretive lens of socially relevant social media 'talk.'"

The character of Gloria Rangaka is played by South African actress Marjorie Langa. Gloria is a single parent of two in her late forties who lives in the township of Soweto and works at Nyathi Family Holdings (NFH) for *The Voice* newspaper as a cleaner. The character of Gloria is important because the bulk of *Scandal!*'s viewership is in townships (Mahlaba, 2023). *Scandal!* wanted to bring to the target market a topic that was not boring. In the episodes under review, Gloria had just come out of an unhappy separation with Abel, the only man she had ever been with in her adult life, and the father of her two children. Prior to meeting Obakeng, Gloria had been married to Abel for 20 years. Abel has been "snatched" by Portia, a rival of Gloria's. According to (Mahlaba, 2023), so *Scandal!* had to make Gloria a relatable woman to both the rich and poor to appeal to all classes of women. Mahlaba (2023) added: "She couldn't be extremely poor so that the rich won't relate or extremely rich that the poor would not relate." Gloria meets Obakeng after unsuccessfully trying to wrest Abel back from Portia. Just as she is about to wed, Abel comes back into her life, asking for forgiveness and wanting her to take him back. However, Gloria decides against this and marries Obakeng. Gloria is a strong matriarch who can hold together a household as a single woman in the township of Soweto, taking care of her children from the proceeds of her job as a cleaner. Gloria loves her family and is very protective of them. Before her marriage to Obakeng, Gloria is a bubbly personality who knows everybody and everything about everybody, an opinionated and vocal, competitive, independent-minded, and ambitious character. This is despite, or over and above, the fact she is a "mere" cleaner. However, Gloria is an object of both fascination and revilement. She seems to be one of those women fated to always be single. In *Black Sexual Politics*, Hill Collins (2004) argues that there are three primary stereotypes of Black women: Mammy (the asexual/deferential caregiver), Jezebel (the manipulative seductress), and Sapphire (the angry, loud, aggressive matriarch). It is interesting that Gloria is all of these in one. She is a fat, desexualised, deferential cleaner/domestic worker who serves the economic interests of the corporate hierarchy of the *Scandal!* newsroom; although not quite a seductress, she is nevertheless manipulative in her social relations; and she is a loud, domineering (though not quite angry and aggressive) matriarch. The Mammy figure is single and works, so she cannot supervise her children, and this contributes to their failure in school and in society. She is single because she is overly aggressive and unfeminine. She emasculates her lovers and husbands, who either refuse to marry her or desert her. All these are images that sustain the sexist, patriarchal, and racist control of Black women. This character and characterisation of Gloria present what Crumpton (2014, p. 4) refers to as a cultural context that violates Black women "through stereotypes and social processes that rendered them simultaneously invincible on one hand and inherently deserving of punishment on the other." In defence of Gloria's characterisation, Mahlaba (2023) points out that they wanted a character that would come back from the abuse she was receiving. They also wanted to show women that it is okay to be stereotyped as there are no easy answers to GBV. She states that *Scandal!* wanted a character that would "bounce back easily" and was "relatable," because it would be upsetting for the audience to see a depressed woman every day. The challenge was: would that characterisation be taken seriously?

Obakeng

The character of Obakeng Rangaka is played by South African actor Peter Moruakgomo. We are introduced to Obakeng as a sales rep and divorcee living alone in Soweto. He is a respected man in the community. He comes to NFH to sell cleaning products, where he meets Gloria and finds love rather unexpectedly. When we first meet him, Obakeng is cast as a nice, if conservative and secretive, guy. He is unassuming, loving, and charming, qualities which sweep Gloria off her feet. The episodes in which he courts her and proposes show him to be a charming and sincere gentleman. He declares his love for Gloria in public, going down on his knee at a Christmas party to say to her:

> Gloria my love, I haven't known you for long, but I do know one thing, I love you and I can't spend another day without you. You complete me. I'm not a young man anymore; I don't have time for games. I want you to be mine forever.

Obakeng claims to have left his ex-wife because she did not love or respect him. He filed for divorce because he claimed that she did not have time for him and always made him feel empty and belittled. Lamia (2013) says that "Those on the rebound are assumed to be distressed, shamed, angry, or sad." She also adds that "Those on the rebound may experience shame and consequently express anger and resentment toward their previous partner." Obakeng appears to fit this profile. It appears that, in Gloria, Obakeng has found the opposite of his ex-wife. At the beginning of their relationship, up to the point of their wedding, Gloria describes Obakeng using the most elevated adjectives. She calls him "spontaneous," "a man who truly loves me, a man who puts me first in his life," and "the sweetest and most loving man I know." Gloria, who left her first husband because of his cheating, was at least expecting that Obakeng would hurt her in the same way and far worse as he would hit her. However, it is not entirely clear that Obakeng is telling the whole truth about the reasons for his divorce. Certainly, his stepdaughter-to-be, Gontse, remains suspicious of him. Obakeng is conflicted because his mother does not like his new wife and refuses either to bless the marriage or to attend the wedding. However, he goes ahead without his mother's blessing, even though it was extremely important to him. Obakeng had even gone back home to Brits to request his uncles to try to persuade his mother to attend the wedding, to no avail. He nearly misses the wedding day because of his attempts to convince his mother to like Gloria.

Both Obakeng and Gloria do not fit into the normative cast and plotline of the soapie since they belong in a lower socio-economic order than the typical *Scandal!* star actors. Neither Gloria nor Obakeng feature in the original plot of *Scandal!* as a soapie about "the newsroom at *The Voice*" and "the lives and beds of the investigative reporters, photographers and editors who will go to any lengths to break the story first."[5] Rather, the two belong in the invisible class of the supporting cast of maintenance workers. According to (Mahlaba, 2023), this was accidental rather than by design. Gloria and Obakeng's romance is thus almost an afterthought in the larger scheme of things of *Scandal!* Obakeng's picture is even missing from the cast roll, suggesting that he is not one of the 22 main characters. This is true, as his character comes and goes. Certainly, in the plotline of *Scandal!*, whatever the likes of Gloria and Obakeng do is meant to be a side-plot. At the time the character of Gloria was conceived, she was the most convenient to use as she had just got divorced and was getting into a new marriage, and this fit in with the GBV plot and the 16 Days of Activism theme. *Scandal!* took us through the marriage stages of courtship, lobola,[6] and then wedding. *Scandal!* pushed this couple to the point of violence. As we will learn in later chapters, these marriage stages are sources of conversation that help to drive the digital media feminist activism that is central to this book. There is so much to talk about around those topics, especially if GBV is involved. The plotline would bring in other hidden aspects, such as property inheritance, the role of people in marriages, and societal expectations of married couples even though a marriage is between two people. Gloria's story was also timely, as noted earlier, because many women murdered by men had been profiled in the media during the same period. She was a favourite of the fans.

Scandal! firstly draws the audience's voyeuristic gaze towards the storyline involving Gloria and Obakeng. As noted, the typical "scandals" of *Scandal!* are those involving the reporters and journalists in the newsroom of *The Voice*, not the cleaners or delivery "boys." Anything centring on the lives of the cleaners or the delivery staff is likely to be seen as a titillating peek into the lives of the "extras," the supporting cast, the "other" and the subaltern of *Scandal!*, bringing with it the same fascination and prurient curiosity that tourists have for the exotic. The drama of gender violence involving Gloria and Obakeng is "exotic" and unusual in the larger scheme of things of *Scandal!* It is a *secondary Scandal!*, a point that allows us to posit a sort of binary between *primary Scandal!* (the main cast of *The Voice*) and *secondary Scandal!* (the cleaners, messengers, delivery boys, and so on). This voyeurism of *secondary Scandal!*, as we will see, shapes some of the social media "talk" we will look at. Such voyeurism-driven social media "talk" has something of the quality that Chase and Levenson in *The Spectacle of Intimacy* (2000, p. 12) call "the eruption of family life into the light of unrelenting public discussion." How much awareness of intimate partner violence *as a social problem* is reflected in the social media "talk" of voyeuristic audiences?

This first point about the voyeuristic social media "talk" leads us to the second point regarding the importance of the side-plot involving Gloria and Obakeng. Normally, the class of domestic workers and gardeners is not thought of as providing proper characters who have fuller, fully fleshed, and rounded lives. Rather, they are often flat characters (the "servants") who are seen in the background, cleaning and delivering things. The violence that ensues between them is not comparable to that of the stars at *The Voice* newspaper. Indeed, "their" marginal violence is not meant to be the focus of our sustained attention. By focusing the spotlight on the margins and making the violence there interesting and worthy of our attention, *Scandal!* mainstreams the topic of gender violence in the "lower" classes that is not normally seen and forces us to reckon with it. Whereas violence against women all too often remains invisible, violence against poor women remains singularly invisible. Das Gupta (1998, p. 210) refers to this as an "attitude of disregard," which frames our readings of "violence in 'Other' women's lives." Indeed, poor women are particularly at risk of victimisation (Belle, 1990; O'Carroll and Mercy, 1986). Obakeng and Gloria bring to *Scandal!* a *domesticity* that is not typical of the *publicity* (or public-ness) of newsroom stars. This domesticity/ publicity binary is critical to the conception of intimacy that is necessary to our later critique of intimate partner violence.

The social media audiences analysed in this book grapple with the way Obakeng turns from charming gentleman to a partner abuser, and the reasons for this transformation. Johnson (1995) identifies two types of intimate partner or couple violence. He calls them "patriarchal terrorism" and "common couple violence." These two types of violence are very different from each other in terms of "the purpose of violence, the frequency at which it occurs, the gendered nature of violence, and the prevalence of it among couples" (Wright, 2011, p. 10).

Patriarchal terrorism is defined as "a product of patriarchal traditions of men's right to control 'their' women," "a form of terroristic control of wives by their husbands that involves the systematic use of not only violence, but economic subordination, threats, isolation, and other control tactics" (Johnson, 1995, p. 284). This kind of violence is always likely to escalate. It is also:

> almost exclusively initiated by the husband, most wives never attempt to fight back, and, among those who do, about one-third quickly desist, leaving only a small minority of cases in which the women respond even with self-defensive violence.
>
> (Johnson, 1995, p. 287)

Common couple violence, on the other hand:

> is less a product of patriarchy, and more a product of the less-gendered causal processes. The dynamic is one in which conflict occasionally gets "out of hand," leading usually to "minor" forms of violence, and more rarely escalating into serious, sometimes even life-threatening, forms of violence.
>
> (Johnson, 1995, p. 285)

That is, common couple violence refers to violence which largely arises from arguments, frustration, or stressors individuals or couples experience (Johnson, 1995; Johnson and Ferraro, 2000). Gloria, as much as Obakeng, could have initiated this kind of violence. Common couple violence, as such, is supposedly an intermittent response to the occasional conflicts of everyday life, motivated by a need to control in the specific situation. Unlike patriarchal terrorism, it does not escalate. Wright (2011, p. 9) points out that, according to social disorganisation theory, structural characteristics of neighbourhoods, such as severe economic "disadvantage," can influence types and rates of intimate partner violence. One factor Obakeng, who typifies male abusers, seems to use is the fact that he dislikes the way Gloria disrespects his mother.

Wright (2011, p. 9) notes that most debate in the literature about intimate partner violence "revolves around whether violence between partners should be measured in terms of the acts or consequences of IPV." Such acts would include hitting or shoving, while consequences refer to the seriousness of injuries inflicted by the violence. The distinction between patriarchal terrorism and common couple violence is critical in our assessment of the nature of social media "talk" about gender violence and the extent to which audiences are aware of these issues.

The abuse of Gloria by Obakeng takes the form of psychological abuse. Obakeng attacks Gloria's self-esteem and confidence by constantly denigrating her. She can never do right in his view. In this episode, he rejects a birthday present that Gloria has thoughtfully prepared for him. Gloria wanted to please him by taking pictures of herself in a low-cut dress that she assumed would be "sexy." Obakeng is visibly unimpressed. He expresses his concern about his wife walking dressed in a low-cut dress. He "accuses" her of vainly trying to look young when it is clear to him that she is no longer young. He is verbally abusive and engages in belittling name-calling. He angrily accuses Gloria of feeding lies to his mother, and intimates that she may be trying to turn mother against son. Gloria is horrified and frightened out of her wits. Seeing that he is so angry, she can hardly defend herself against the torrent of verbal abuse. She tries, instead, to calm him down and placate him. She also appears to believe that if she accepts all the blame, Obakeng will calm down.

At one point, Gloria gets angry and talks back. This is after telling Obakeng that she does not accept his mentioning of her daughter in a disparaging way. Obakeng retaliates by threatening to sell the house. Gloria objects, and says to him: "You will do no such thing. This is my house!" This is too much for Obakeng, who slaps Gloria hard across the face, and hurts her rather badly (Figure 1.1). He then warns her not to push his buttons any further. This is a first for Gloria; she never expected that a man would hit her, more so one she

Figure 1.1 Obakeng slaps Gloria (Source: Kashan Krawitz)

loved. She does not scream or run to the neighbours, but decides to bear the violence. She does not want people to know what is going on, as she is flushed with shame and fear. Obakeng, who seems to realise what he has done, begs Gloria not to tell people about the real cause of her injuries (Figure 1.2). When she calls the police on him, he instructs her to lie to them about the abuse, and instead say that she was the victim of an accidental fall. She obliges. Obakeng also goes ahead with the process of trying to sell the house, despite Gloria's objections and despite the house not belonging to him. The issue of the house is central to the abuse, since Obakeng feels emasculated by living in his wife's house. Selling it is his way of getting even. At the same time, although he often says sorry, Obakeng also feels that he is right to abuse Gloria to make her more loyal and submissive.

Gloria keeps the information of the escalating abuse to herself. She seems to believe that Obakeng will change for the better, or else blames herself for the fact that she is not a "perfect wife." The fact that Obakeng sometimes becomes contrite and apologises gives her hope that he might change for the better. After hitting her, he says he is sorry and promises never to do it again. Gloria also shudders to think what will happen when the community of Soweto hears that she is being abused after such a splendid wedding (Figure 1.3).

Figure 1.2 Gloria's bruised and battered face (Source: Kashan Krawitz)

Figure 1.3 Gloria and Obakeng's "special" wedding (Source: Kashan Krawitz)

She prefers that everyone mind their own business. Her excessive pride makes her refuse to admit the severity of the abuse or accept offers of help. Finally, she knows that Obakeng wants her to be submissive and loyal. She thus blames herself for her disloyalty and lack of submissiveness. She wishes she were more submissive and loyal, then perhaps the abuse would stop. She remembers, for instance, the incident when she wrongly suspected Obakeng of having a lover when he was only sneaking out to be with his mother.

Basically, it is possible that Gloria may have continued to entertain the hope that Obakeng might change. Jordan et al. (2004, p. 15) suggest that "fear of the offender and the risk of harm to which he exposes the victim may influence a woman to remain in the violent relationship." Ellard, Herbert, and Thompson (1991) suggest that women stay in abusive relationships partly because they are emotionally attached to the relationship. Gloria had already seen a previous marriage fail, had been cheated on, had seen Abel walk out on her, and had faced many imponderables. It is possible that she contemplated various courses of action. The point to be emphasised here is that in Gloria and Obakeng's relationship, violence and love *traverse* each other in complex, ineffable ways. The tension between violence and intimacy appears to have affected Gloria and made her put up with violence and insults longer than she should have.

For instance, she has been going behind Obakeng's back since he hit her and started the process of putting up the house for sale. However, she is still not thinking clearly about what is going on in her life. Obakeng had hit her repeatedly until she called the police on him. Because no one opposes him, Obakeng gets into the habit of abusing Gloria at every turn. Her life has become a living hell. Complicating the abuse is not only the fact that Gloria blames herself, but that she is proud, trapped, and never expected a toxic relationship. Having discovered for the first time that she is a bona fide victim of domestic abuse via the "epiphany" of the first slap, Gloria gradually starts to fight back.

When Obakeng finds out that Gloria has a helper to assist her with household chores, he gets angry and tells Gloria that he feels deeply disrespected. He tells her that a proper wife cooks meals for her husband instead of outsourcing this duty. At this stage, the community decides to act. The men of Soweto take drastic action and manhandle Obakeng, who is arrested and sent to prison. He phones Gloria from his jail cell and pleads with her to testify in his favour. She refuses. Escalation of the abuse thus happens not only because of inaction from both Gloria's side and the community's side, but because the abuse happened to act like a slow poison and had many levels. It took the escalation to physical abuse for it to reach a turning point.

The cycle of violence follows a pattern more or less in this form: an incident occurs that builds tension, and an argument ensues; it is followed by the abusive stage, which is verbal, emotional, physical, or sexual. This stage can last for minutes or days. After the abusive stage comes to a honeymoon stage where the abuser apologises, proclaims love, buys gifts, and promises not to do it again. As the relationship progresses, the abuse gets worse, and the intervals grow shorter and do not progress to the honeymoon stage anymore. The abuser no longer apologises or cares. Some unlucky women never go past the last abusive stage; they end up dead. Some are killed the moment they decide to end the relationship (Ackroyd, 2015). By refusing to open the door for Obakeng when he came home in a murderous mood pretending to want to apologise, Gloria probably escaped death by a whisker. Gelles (2017, p. 20) opines that "physical violence is the ultimate resource that can be utilized to hold subordinate groups in place."

Kelly and Radford (1996) note that some women tend to rationalise, trivialise, and minimise their abuse, often saying "but nothing really happened" or "but nothing actually happened" after abusive comments/threats, unwanted physical contact, or attempted or actual sexual assault. It is a worryingly common behaviour for some women to initially, or even permanently, accept abuse. For some reason, some abused women feel that "it can't be that bad." At the same time, there are complicating factors that prevent abused women from leaving, such as lack of financial means, isolation (such as the abuser preventing her from seeing other people), threats to harm people she cares for, and the community refusing to believe her. There is also the fear of the unknown, such as the fear that the man will kill her if she leaves, numbness and paralysis, and low self-esteem and a sense of worthlessness. hooks (1982, p. 7) even suggests, worryingly, that when a woman perseveres in an oppressive situation, it may be because she is used to being oppressed. She warns that to be strong in the face of oppression is not the same as overcoming oppression. Apparently, Black women are socialised or conditioned to "adjust, adapt and cope."

Societal factors, such as shame, stigma, and embarrassment, the presence of children, and the need to protect the partner may prevent the victim from leaving. There are also complex emotional factors that come into play, such as "love" for the abuser, or the belief that he will change if she stays and tries hard enough. Gloria for a long time overlooked and underplayed the psychological abuse meted out to her by Obakeng. The depression and post-traumatic stress she experienced did not seem to her to count as domestic violence. Poet, author, and activist Maya Angelou, who suffered domestic abuse, points out some of the emotional traumas triggered by domestic violence which victims may have to live with: depression, anxiety, panic attacks, substance abuse, and post-traumatic stress disorder (PTSD), which can lead to suicide attempts, psychotic episodes, and even homelessness.[7] Gloria "solves" the problem by keeping away from and avoiding her close friends and neighbours. She wants to keep the abuse a secret at all costs. At work is the paralysis brought on by stigma that Pizzey (1974) wrote of in her book on partner abuse, *Scream Quietly or the Neighbors Will Hear*. Gloria was certainly attempting to scream quietly so that the people of Soweto would not hear. Even Obakeng complaining about Gloria's friends was a way of isolating her. She was also paralysed by fear of the social stigma of not being married, and the fear of being alone. Certainly, there is a case that can be made for arguing that Gloria was paralysed by a fear of being without a partner.

Obakeng's controlling, domineering, and manipulative behaviours appear to arise from many sources. Partly, he is jealous and paranoid. He is jealous and paranoid because he does not trust his wife. He does not trust his wife because, although they love each other, they are both strangers at the level of intimacy. Another reason for Obakeng's controlling, abusive nature is that he is a conservative man who resents being married to an independent, ambitious woman. He prefers Gloria to be loyal and submissive. His insecurities, however, also show another side to Obakeng. He is not just a victim of passion. By not wanting his wife to make some money for herself by holding tripe nights, and by wanting to sell the house, he is selfish and insensitive. His behaviour in belittling his wife and treating her like a child shows the other side of his nature. He seems deliberately controlling and manipulative. Finally, Obakeng is a chameleon. Although he played the charmer in the early days of his relationship with Gloria, research into his previous marriage shows that he has a history of intimate partner abuse. A leopard does not change its spots. It is not clear, however, to what extent he is in control of his actions. On one level, although he seems to realise that what he is doing to Gloria is wrong, it seems he cannot stop himself. Throughout the abuse, Obakeng would still call Gloria his "Sunflower." He seems as much trapped as Gloria, or at least incapable of seeing himself self-reflexively as an abuser. Unfortunately, the producers of *Scandal!* did not explain exactly what the source of Obakeng's problem was, or how an abuser like him could be rehabilitated. On another level, however, Obakeng's actions betray agency and culpability. His ability to manipulate Gloria to lie to the police and to her children and neighbours, and his lying about his previous relationship, suggest that he knows what he is doing.

Knowing these forms of violence helps to understand digital media feminist activism and its importance. What we see manifesting as beating or murder of women would have gone through some of these GBV cycles. That is why this book brings in the aspect of the death of Uyinene, who is a symbol of #AmINext in South Africa. The daily murder of women in South Africa has heightened the concept of digital media feminist activism, which is helping people overcome to the private nature of GBV. Gloria epitomises violence against women in the marginalised communities, and Obakeng represents the nature of male abusers in the country. The drama that plays out between Obakeng and Gloria is reflected in real life on the #AmINext hashtag, where audiences post comments about real murders of women, mostly by their intimate partners. Feminists continue to wrestle with GBV, and an analysis of the manufacture of fear in next section will give us insights to how the GBV problem manifests.

The manufacture of female fear

Gender violence speaks to the broader global feminist politics, and understanding its genealogy is vital. Scholars such as Löwstedt (2015) have traced the genealogy of violence against women to apartheid, calling it a historical issue (2012; Gqola, 2015; Lowstedt, 2015).[8] Feminists such as Gqola (2015, p. 79) blame the rising cases of GBV in South Africa on what they call "the manufacture of female fear," which is a historical phenomenon that uses "the threat of rape and other bodily wounding." The argument is that female bodies have faced very specific forms and genealogies of wounding, surveillance, control, punishment, mutilation, and structural violence reproduced by successive forms of patriarchy, sexism, and misogyny. These are similar to the issues which years later the digital media feminist activism against GBV is still fighting. Historically, such violence against female bodies was specifically built into slavery, empire, colonialism, and apartheid as part of a generalised violence against Black bodies (Gqola, 2015, p. 45). It has, however, metamorphosed into a variety of forms, some old and some new. In the "new" South Africa, for instance, bodily wounding of women takes the form of femicide. Lowstedt (2015) defines femicide as "the intentional targeting of women and girls with lethal force because they are girls and women." This point is still relevant for South African women and girls who still daily experience GBV.

Incidentally, there is no one single type of violence against women. Fear is manufactured, for instance, through threats of physical harm, denial, or deprivation of financial resources, an attitude of excessive surveillance and possessiveness, and other behaviours of control that result in women suffering a loss of self-worth, dignity and self-esteem, confidence, and independence (Mega, Mega, Mega, and Harris, 2000).

The manufacture of female fear requires several aspects to work: the safety of the aggressor, the vulnerability of the target, and the successful communication by the aggressor that he has the power to wound, rape, and/or kill the target with no consequences to himself. Women are socialised to look away from the female fear factory – to pretend it is not happening, and to flee when ignoring it becomes impossible. Patriarchy trains us all to be receptive to the conditions that produce – and reproduce – female fear, especially when it is not our own bodies on the assembly line (Gqola, 2015, p. 80).

Complicating how VAW is talked about on online spaces and how it extends to the manufacture of fear is the response of certain men's rights movements who believe "feminism is the enemy." There has been an emergence of the so-called "manosphere,"[9] a "collection of websites, Facebook pages, and chat rooms where men vent their rage and spew anti-women rhetoric" (Pry and Valiente, 2013). Wiseman (2014) contends that the manosphere is where men from mixed backgrounds, some of them victims of abuse, and father's rights proponents believe women are designed solely for sex.[10] These men are so daring because they are protected by the anonymity offered by online spaces (Pry and Valiente, 2013). However, this anonymity has also transferred power to women, who can speak out without fear of being identified and physically attacked. Men who practise the manosphere do it for attention because they feel the courts are biased against them and they are not getting a fair deal. They also do this to influence policy (Pry and Valiente, 2013).[11]

Yet women contend that they encounter violence against them by men everywhere.[12] Wiseman expands on these claims:

> Every woman I know has been shouted at by a stranger, has been called a whore, bitch, or slut, whispered to, hissed at, threatened, pressed against, rubbed. Some women I know have been physically attacked, some haven't ... Every woman I know has been warned about walking back in the dark, even though they know that most acts of violence happen at home, by somebody they know; every woman I know has carried their keys spiked through their knuckles when they walk down the road at night. Every woman I know texts their friends to say they're home safe.[13]

Wiseman further postulates that attacks on women by men continue in cyberspaces, such as in emails and social media.[14] Men practising the manosphere deny they are anti-women, but argue that they are simply documenting how they feel. Iqbal (2018), who has been exploring online antifeminism since 2015, points out that these men feel justified. Iqbal further contends that there is no way of telling if these misogynists are all men due to the anonymity of online space, which is true of what *Scandal!* and the hashtag #AmINext reveal.[15]

Apart from challenges brought about by the manosphere, fighting GBV has proved troublesome because women are not subjected to violence for the same reasons or in the same ways (Zuckerhut, 2011). On the surface, it might appear that a perpetrator such as Obakeng initiates abuse *spontaneously*. For instance, he may feel that the victim did not behave appropriately or did not fulfil her duties, and thus had to be punished (Zuckerhut, 2011). However, the likes of Gqola and Lowstedt (2015) and Sibanda-Moyo et al. (2017) caution that looking at surface causes or failing to consider the interplay of history and structural factors can lead us to depend on superficial explanations. Sibanda-Moyo et al. (2017, p. 5), for instance, blame high incidences of violence against women in South Africa on socio-economic factors that include women's limited education, capital, labour opportunities, and resource control, the culture of violence in South Africa that was inherited from the violent pasts of apartheid, colonialism, and empire, and the culture of silence.

What is also important to observe in relation to patriarchy, as we learn how audiences respond to GBV through new media platforms, is that specific intervening psychological variables are believed to also be important in the study of domestic violence. That is where feminism is key to help us understand how patriarchy feeds into GBV. Tifft (1993) points to research designed to discover correlates of men who batter women. These men have difficulty in forming close relationships, commonly express negative emotion through anger, and possess diminished self-esteem (Pagelow, 1984, p. 81). They hold patriarchal, sex-stereotyped values, subscribe to rigid sex role definitions, and believe that society sanctions controlling women and keeping them in a position subordinate to men (Watts and Courtois, 1981, p. 246). They believe in violence against wives they perceive as violating the ideals of family patriarchy. They consistently express jealousy and do not recognise the real effects of their violence, have often been exposed to violence as children, and often exhibit stress symptoms from work, family, and financial pressures. They have difficulty in maintaining intimate relationships because they fear intimacy and have a high need for control and power. However, it is not conclusive whether these attributes result in battering (Tifft,1993, p. 11). Correlation does not prove causation. Many of these attributes are also present in men and women in "highly distressed or discordant relationships" regardless of whether battering is present or not. That is, the research does not tell us much about *why* violence by men is directed towards a selected specific target – for instance, women/intimate partners within a specific selected context, which in this case is the household (Schechter, 1982, pp. 210–211).

Knowing about these types of research helps books such as this one, which are expanding on the present knowledge about GBV by focusing on less known social media platforms and what people say on those platforms. For example, feminists have established that although not all physical or sexual violence is a result of patriarchal power, it is considered a major contributor (Holter, 1984). In South Africa, the patriarchal system is embedded in society regardless of race or class (Pillay, 2010, p. 66.) Physical violence is thus associated with power relations. Tifft postulates that when men physically batter their partners, this behaviour serves as an enforcer of men's exercise of institutional and personal power. Are these meanings the same in this digital media feminist activism era?

Ayiera (2010, p. 13) argues that violence against women is a "prominent expression of pattern[s] of domination." Subordination of women is legitimised through the hierarchal structure of the family unit, as well as the institutions and social structure of society (Sigler, 1989), such that women are considered "appropriate victims." Hence:

> Patriarchy as a social-political order is based on male hegemony through dominance and denigration of other experiences. It concentrates power at public and private spheres within the male. "Normal" is defined from the perspective of the heterosexual male and other perspectives are peripheral ... Violence is an acceptable and integral part of maintaining this order, insofar as it does not fundamentally threaten the structures.
> (Ayiera, 2010, pp. 12–13)

Dealing with patriarchy requires attacking it at its roots, and digital media activism is a vehicle that people can use to do this. It is, for instance, creating spaces for equal gender representation and integrating interventions that transform the lives of women socially, educationally, and economically. Traditional or conservative gender attitudes are regarded by some as stemming from the belief that men and women's roles are clearly demarcated. For example, girls must be "submissive" or "docile," while boys should be "aggressive" and "dominating" (York, 2011, p. 15). Willis (1992) observes that people who uphold these conservative attitudes are likely to blame female victims of violence. Perpetrators may, in such cases, get communal support or sympathy for their actions. Digital media feminist activism is helping to question such attitudes. It is also playing a critical role in education, for instance to emancipate women and prevent abuse. Communication strategists insist that the media plays a key role in shaping perceptions. Sibanda-Moyo et al. (2017, p. 68) state that:

> Messages conveyed through the media often determine whether survivors speak out about their abuse, and the nature of support and

assistance women receive from the public and the criminal justice system. Therefore, while the media may be influential in promoting negative ideas about VAW, it also has the power to be part of the solution.

Violence against women, although blamed on patriarchy, is also believed to stem from other disparate sources (Lowstedt, 2015). Some theories, for instance, suggest as causes mental illness, abuse of alcohol, drug and other substance abuse; socio-economic deprivation and social isolation, poverty, educational and age gaps, and cultural practices (Kurst-Swanger and Petcosky, 2003, pp. 34–35). In some cases, family violence is fostered and maintained due to a society's general acceptance of violence as a normative and legitimate means of resolving conflict (Tifft, 1993, p. 1). Gqola (2015, p. 45), in her study of the example of rape, cautions against taking the view that rape is merely a manifestation of contemporary post-apartheid "culture." Rape, rather, has a specific and traceable genealogy. For instance, rape can be traced back to the "architecture of slave-ordered Cape Colony" (Gqola, 2015, p. 40). The history of rape "is the history of slavery, colonialism and race science" (p. 40). Indeed, South Africa itself was founded on the "trauma of slavery and sexual subjection" (pp. 42–43). Historically, the violation of Black bodies was the norm. Such norms are still with us today, which makes the topic of this book relevant. The structure of this book has been designed to help us understand the connection between GBV and the role of digital media activism and feminist politics.

Book structure

Methodologically, the book is based on data obtained using a qualitative netnography study. This method is unique, in that those who do traditional ethnography necessarily venture into the world "out there" (the "outside"), while netnographers only travel virtually, with their bums on seats (the "inside"). The old image of ethnography as an immersive practice appeals to the netnographers and is important in their self-image. Netnography is fairly a new tool of research, developed in the mid-1990s, following the emergence of the nascent field of online research pioneered by Nancy Baym in the early 1990s (Hine, 2008, p. 922).

The research regarded whatever was posted by individuals on Facebook about Gloria and Obakeng or on the #AmINext hashtag as constituting "talk," whether it was a word, words, series of letters, punctuation marks, an emoticon, or emoji. At the same time, individuals are unique, so it was not just the description of what they said and how they said it that the research was interested in. Rather, it was also interested in theorising what lurked behind what they said. This is where feminist theory helped to interpret whatever was being uttered.

The discursive approach that gives us social media "talk" as a unit of study and a unit of analysis ensures that we are still preoccupied with "weighty" political themes such as gender violence. They do not go away just because we are studying social media. We are not just describing strings of text or comments. The aim of the study that informs this book was to lead us to a "better understanding" of society, gendered attitudes, and "improvements in practice." Such data assists in filling a void in existing literature and helps to establish a new line of thinking. The success of this book, whether or not it is framed as a political project, rests on its not being minimised by the fact that I scraped my "data" from Facebook and Twitter instead of interviewing "real" South African women who experience intimate partner violence. If anything, there was a lot to learn from this data. The next section contextualises the limitations of the book.

Limitations

Social media "talk" results from a give-and-take between the so-called "real world" and the online world – in this case, Facebook and Twitter. The phenomenon would not be possible without either of the two worlds. Facebook, for instance, was seen in this book as a constrained platform for connecting *Like-minded* people. I use the word "Like-minded" with a capital "L" not only because the participants all like the same soap opera, *Scandal!*, but because they click the Facebook "Like" button. The conceptual genealogy of such a group is worth commenting on. It is because of *Scandal!* that this group exists on Facebook in the first place. That is, members of the fan group do not like the soap opera *because* of Facebook. Rather, before there is social media, there is a prior fact of the existence of a community of a television audience, dispersed across South Africa and beyond, which watches *Scandal!* Social media weaves together these audiences, and allows them to speak to, with, and against one another. So the fact that all the participants watch, and "love" *Scandal!* fosters a feeling of connectedness and brings a sense of community that is *prior* to their use of social media. In this book, the culture of television watching merges with the online community of Facebook groups. Netnography itself revolves around those two terms: "culture" and "community" (Kozinets, 2010, p. 5).

Without social media, the sense of community we refer to is more imagined than real. Indeed, it is, in a sense, impossible – unless people meet physically to discuss their viewing of the soapie. The community is linked together by each member clicking the "Like" button of the "Fans of Scandal" Facebook page or Twitter followers of the #AmINext hashtag. The "Like" button enables this community to *come into being* as a Facebook "group" or as Twitter followers. Through Facebook groups or Twitter followers rallying around a particular hashtag, members can post content. Through the mediation of the "Like" button, fans of *Scandal!* or Twitter followers of the #AmINext can interact with comments, emojis, and photos. For example, once fans of *Scandal!* click the "Like" button, as the researcher did to be part of the group, they were able to see displays of the number of other *Scandal!* fans who "Liked" the content. This display included a full or partial list of those *Scandal!* fans. In a sense, therefore, social media "talk" is enabled by Facebook's "Like" button.

Users can comment only after they have "Liked" the page, just as one needs to follow or visit a hashtag to comment on Twitter. This is part of the internal geography and architecture of Facebook and Twitter, constructed around algorithms and strict "Terms of Service" and "Community Standards."[16] For example, any community that participates in social media "talk" on Facebook not only needs to use the "Like" button, but must adhere to Facebook's "Terms of Service." So if someone loves *Scandal!* but does not want to "Like" the show on Facebook and does not want to adhere to Facebook's "Terms of Service," they will not get a chance to "talk" on social media. If someone "talks" in a way that breaches Facebook's "Community Standards," they will be banned from social media "talk." Even when someone has permission to communicate on Facebook, their very means and techniques of communication are constrained by Facebook's tools and features. For instance, if someone needs to react to something, they cannot just react in any way they like, but rather, need to long-press the "Like" button. By long-pressing the "Like" button, they get the option to use one of five pre-defined emotions: "Love," "Care," "Haha," "Wow," "Sad," or "Angry." These options exist because Facebook does not allow its users to dislike content. Users are only allowed to Like things. If someone intends to express an emotion, they can only do so via the emoji picker provided by Facebook or choose from the available Facebook GIFs. They cannot, for instance, upload their own GIFs. There is thus a myriad of built-in limitations to any form of social media "talk."

Fuchs, in the chapter "Social Media as Ideology" in *Social Media: A Critical Introduction* (2017), argues there is nothing innocent in Facebook's "Like" button. Rather, the whole architecture is infused with power and ideology, and renders us powerless and exploited. He asserts that, in fact, Facebook advances "an ideology of liking" in the form of its "Like" button. We must thus be constantly alive to the political economy of Facebook, including its surveillance projects. I broadly concur with Fuchs. Once someone is part of a group, and if they adhere to Facebook rules, they can "speak" on social media. There are few rules about how one can "talk" once one is ensconced in, and sutured to, Facebook's algorithms. People can say what they want (again, if what they say does not breach Facebook rules). Social media "talk" can be formal or informal, consequential or useless, weighty conversation or a noticeboard for small "talk" chit-chat. All this was on show on the *Scandal!* fans' Facebook page. It is this multiform and intuitive conversation that offers significant insights, knowledge, and meanings in our awareness of social issues such as gender violence.

Adding to the limitations is the fact that internet access and connectivity in Africa are constrained due to infrastructure problems such as availability of fibre optics or any other technology reception structures such as in remote areas, high data costs, and costs of digital technology devices. Some 16 million South Africans out of a population of 60 million are on Facebook. There is a likelihood that this "talk" was elitist, and out of bounds to many who were not on Facebook and Twitter or who had no internet access.

There is a worldwide tendency to buy followers, real or imagined, although both Facebook and Twitter make efforts to clean out all fake accounts. This distorts the definition of the audience.

Scandal! is viewed mostly by adults aged 25–50 years, 60 per cent of whom are women (Gaines, 2015). In addition to the fact that *Scandal!* has been showing on e-television (etv) for over a decade, the soap opera genre gives viewers something to "talk" about because of the way soaps are structured – for instance, the "endless narratives" (Brunsdon, 2000, p. 173). The study of soap operas as a genre has been centred on the texts or as part of television studies. This book offers an insight into the role of the soap opera in the digital era. It allows us to examine soaps' function as an auxiliary tool that is helping to extend conversations about GBV from social television to multimedia digital platforms, thereby helping us to learn what the audience thinks about it. McQuail (2010, p. 548) observes that by focusing on social issues, the media has the potential to highlight the importance and relation of social media to social change. This was part of the thinking behind etv's producers creating the episodes that represented violence against women that informs this book.

The book is divided into five chapters. Chapter 1 lays out an introduction that sets the scene, providing the background on VAW in South Africa, summarising *Scandal!* episodes, discussing the manufacture of female fear, and setting out the structure of the book. Chapter 2 centres on GBV and digital technologies. Chapter 3 discusses GBV as a broader feminist political problem. Chapter 4 gives us the gender digital activism perspective and its relevance to GBV, describing the nature of social media "talk." Chapter 5 describes the audiences and language and their implications for digital gender activism in relation to GBV.

Notes

1 WHO (n.d.) "Intimate partner violence and alcohol", Accessed 4 May 2018.
2 Willis, A. (18 May 2017) "Media reports would have you believe there is an Increase gender-based violence, but there Isn't. Less than 20 percent of all femicides that happen every year are covered in the press". *Huffington Post*, https://www.huffingtonpost.co.uk/entry/media-reports-would-have-you-believe-there-is-an-increase-gender_uk_5c7ea7e3e4b078abc6c22858. Accessed 10 April 2018.
3 September, C. (31 October 2013) "The Anene Booysen story". *Eyewitness News*, https://ewn.co.za/2013/10/31/The-Anene-Booysen-Story. Accessed 15 September 2016.
4 Alter, C. (25 November 2014) "The brutal triple murder behind the International Day for the Elimination of Violence Against Women". *TIME*, http://time.com/3603582/international-day-to-end-violence-against-women/. Accessed 22 November 2018.

5 SCANDAL! is a true melting pot of South African life depicted through the heightened and entertaining genre of soap in which its villains and heroes play out the complex twists and turns of their lives in their home, business and recreational environments. The url is https://www.etv.co.za/shows/scandal.
6 It is the provision of gifts to the parents of a bride, usually in the form of cash or livestock. Culturally if this is not done the union is considered as cohabitation or prostitution. Mangena, T., & Ndlovu, S. 2013. Implications and Complications of Bride price Payment among the Shona and Ndebele of Zimbabwe. *International Journal of Asian Social Science*, 3(2), 472–481. Retrieved from https://archive.aessweb.com/index.php/5007/article/view/2431
7 Children exposed to domestic violence are also at risk of developmental problems, psychiatric disorders, school difficulties, aggressive behaviour, and low self-esteem.
8 Abrahams, N., Mathews, S., Martin, L., Lombard, C., & Jewkes, R. (1 August 2012) "Every eight hours: Intimate femicide in South Africa 10 years later!". saMRC, https://www.mrc.ac.za/policy-briefs/every-eight-hours-intimate-femicide-south-africa-10-years-later/. Accessed 10 December 2017.
9 Pry, A., & Valiente, A. (15 October 2013) "Women battle online anti-women hate from the 'manosphere'". ABC News, https://abcnews.go.com/Technology/women-battle-online-anti-women-hate-manosphere/story?id=20579038. Accessed 12 December 2018.
10 Wiseman, E. (1 June 2014) "The everyday fear of violence every woman has to cope with". *The Guardian*, https://www.theguardian.com/lifeandstyle/2014/jun/01/mens-rights-internet-forums-distance-from-misogynist-mass-murder. Accessed 12 December 2018.
11 Iqbal, N. (11 November 2018) "Social media has elevated misogyny to new levels of violence". *The Guardian*, https://www.theguardian.com/books/2018/nov/11/donna-zuckerberg-social-media-misoyny-violence-classical-antiquity-not-all-dead-white-men. Accessed 11 November 2018.
12 Ibid.
13 Wiseman, "The everyday fear of violence every woman has to cope with".
14 Ibid.
15 Iqbal, "Social media has elevated misogyny to new levels of violence".
16 Facebook has six "Community Standards", covering: (i) violence and criminal behaviour, (ii) safety, (iii), objectionable content, (iv) integrity and authenticity, (v) respecting intellectual property, and (vi) content-related requests. https://www.facebook.com/communitystandards/introduction.

References

Abrahams, N., Mathews, S., Jewkes, R., Martin, L.J., & Lombard, C. (2012). *Every eight hours: Intimate femicide in South Africa 10 years later*. Cape Town: University of Cape Town.

Ackroyd, B. (2015). INFOGRAPHIC: Domestic violence in SA. Home page. http://www.enca.com/south-africa/infographic-domestic-violence-sa. Accessed 2018/05/21.

Antrobus, P. (2004). *The global women's movement: Origins, issues and strategies*. New York: St Martins Press.

Ayiera, E. (2010). Sexual violence in conflict: A problematic international discourse. *Feminist Africa Issue*, 14, 7–18.

Belle, D. (1990). Poverty and women's mental health. *American Psychologist*, 45, 385–389.

Brunsdon, C. (2000). *The feminist, the housewife and the soap opera*. Oxford: Clarendon press.
Burton, N. (2012). South African soapies. A "rainbow nation" realised? In Smith-Shomade, B.E. (Ed), *Watching while black: Centering the television of black audiences*. London: Rutgers University Press, pp. 220–231.
Carrillo, R. (1991). Violence against women: An obstacle for development. In Bunch, C., & Carrillo, R. (Ed), *Gender violence: A development and human rights issue*. New York: Centre for Women's Global Leadership, p. 42.
Chase, K., & Levenson, M. (2000). *The spectacle of intimacy*. Princeton, NJ: Prince University Press.
Crumpton, S.M. (2014). *A womanist pastoral theology against intimate and cultural violence*. New York: Palgrave.
Das Gupta, S. (1998). Women's realities: Defining violence against women by immigration, race, and class. In Bergen, R.A. (Ed), *Issues in intimate violence*. New York: Sage, pp. 209–219.
Ellard, J.H., Herbert, T.B., & Thompson, L.J. (1991). Coping with an abusive relationship: How and why do people stay? *Journal of Marriage and the Family*, 53, 311–325.
Ennaji, M., & Sadiqi, F. (2011). Introduction: Contextualising gender and violence in the Middle East. In Ennaji, M., & Sadiqi, F. (Eds), *Gender and violence in the Middle East*, London: Routledge, pp. 1–9.
Fuchs, C. (2017). *Social media: A critical introduction* (Second Edition). London: Sage.
Gaines, L. (2015). Email interview. Johannesburg. 20 August. Email notes available from the author.
Gqola, D.P. (2015). *Rape: A South African nightmare*. Johannesburg: JM Books.
Gelles, R.J. (2017). *Intimate violence and abuse in families*. New York: Oxford university Press.
Hester, M., Kelly, L., & Radford, J. (1996). *Women, violence and male power*. Oxford: Oxford University Press.
Hill Collins, P. (2004). *Black sexual politics: African Americans, gender, and the new racism*. London: Routledge.
Hine, C.M. (2008). Virtual ethnography. In Given, L. (Ed), *The Sage encyclopedia of qualitative research methods*, Volumes 1&2. London: Sage, pp. 921–924.
Holter, H. (1984). Women's research and social theory. In Holter, H. (Ed), *Patriarchy in a welfare society*. Irvington-on-Hudson, NY: Columbia University Press, pp. 9–25.
hooks, bell. (1982). *Ain't I a woman: Black women and feminism*. Boston: South End Press.
Izumi, K. (2007). Gender based violence and property grabbing in Africa: A denial of women's liberty and security. In Terry, G., & Hoare J. (Eds), *Gender-based violence*, pp. 14–25.
Joachim, J.M. (2007). *Agenda setting, the UN, and the NGOs: Gender violence and reproductive rights*. Washington, DC: Georgetown University Press.
Johnson, M. (1995). Patriarchal terrorism and common couple violence: Two forms of violence against women. *Journal of Marriage and Family*, 57, 283–294. 10.2307/353683.

Johnson, M.P., & Ferraro, K. (2000). Research on domestic violence in the 1990s: Making distinctions. *Journal of Marriage and the Family*, 62, 948–963.

Jordan, C.E., Nietzel, M.T., Walker, R., & Logan, T.K. (2004). *Intimate partner violence: A clinical training guide for mental health professionals*. New York: Springer.

Kozinets, R.V. (2010). *Netnography: Doing ethnographic research online*. London: Sage.

Kurst-Swanger, K., & Petcosky, J.L. (2003). *Violence in the home: Multidisciplinary perspectives*. New York: Oxford University Press.

Lamia, M.C. (2013). Rebound relationships. https://www.psychologytoday.com/us/blog/intense-emotions-and-strong-feelings/201309/rebound-relationships

Lowstedt, A. (2015). Femicide in Apartheid: The parallel interplay between racism and sexism in South Africa and Palestine-Israel. In Ilan, P. (Ed), *Israel and South Africa: The many faces of apartheid*. London: Zed Books, pp. 191–238.

Mahlaba, G. (2023). WhatsApp interview. Johannesburg. 14 February. Interview notes available from the author.

McQuail, D. (2010). *McQuail's mass communication theory*. London: Sage.

Mega, L.T., Mega, J.L., Mega, B.T., & Harris, B.M. (2000). Brainwashing and battering fatigue: Psychological abuse in domestic violence. *North Carolina Medical Journal*, 61(5), 260–265.

Mogale, S.R., Barns, K.K., & Ritcher, S. (2012). Violence against women in South Africa: Policy position and recommendations. *Violence Against Women*, 18(5), 580–594.

National strategic plan on gender-based violence and femicide. (2020). https://www.samrc.ac.za/sites/default/files/files/2020-05-11/NSPGenderBasedVF.pdf493090

O'Carroll, P.W., & Mercy, J.A. (1986). Patterns and recent trends in black homicide. In Hawkins, D.F. (Ed.), *Homicide among black Americans*. Lanham, MD: University Press of America, 29–42.

Pizzey, E. (1974). *Scream quietly or the neighbours will hear*. Berkeley Heights, NJ: Enslow Publishing.

Pagelow, M.D. (1984). *Family violence*. New York: Praeger.

Pillay, A. (2010). Women's activism and transformation: Arising from the cusp. *Feminist Africa*, 14, 63–78.

Rushton, J.P. (1982). Television and prosocial behaviour. In Pearl, D., Bouthilet, L., & Lazar, J. (Eds), *Television and behaviour*, Volume 2 Technical Review. Washington, DC: National Institute of Mental Health, pp. 248–257.

Schechter, S. (1982). *Women and male violence: The visions and struggles of the battered women's movement*. Boston: South End Press.

Sibanda-Moyo, N., Konje, E., & Brobbey, M.K. (2017). *Violence against women in South Africa: A country in crisis 2017*. Johannesburg: Centre for the Study of Violence and Reconstruction.

Sigler, R.T. (1989). *Domestic violence in context: An assessment of community attitudes*. Lexington, MA: Lexington Books.

Smith, J. (2005). 16 days of peace. Home page. http://www.waccglobal.org/en/resources/media-and-gender-monitor/98-issue-12/1019-16-Days-of-Peace.html. Accessed 2011/09/06.

Spence, L. (2001). "They killed off Marlena, but she's on another show now": Fantasy, reality, and pleasure in watching daytime soap operas. In Allen, R.C. (Ed), *To be continued...soap operas around the world*. London: Routledge, pp. 182–198.

Tifft, L.R. (1993). *Battering of women: The failure of intervention and the case for prevention.* Oxford: Westview Press.

Watts, D.I., & Courtois, C.A. (1981). Trends in the treatment of men who commit violence against women. *Personal and Guidance Journal,* 60, 245–249.

Willis, C.E. (1992). The effect of sex role stereotype, victim and defendant race, and prior relationship on rape culpability attributions. *Sex Roles,* 26, 213–226.

Wies, R.J., Haldane, H.J. (2011). Ethnographic notes from the front lines of gender-based violence. In Wies, R.J., Haldane, H.J. (Eds), *Anthropology at the front lines of gender-based violence.* Nashville, TN: Vanderbilt University Press, pp. 1–18.

Wright, E.M. (2011). *Neighborhoods and Intimate Partner Violence.* El Paso: LFB Scholarly Publishing LLC.

York, M.R. (2011). *Gender attitudes and violence against women.* New York: LFB Scholarly Publishing LLC.

Zizek, S. (2007). Censorship Today: Violence, or Ecology as a New Opium for the Masses. Home page. http://www.lacan.com/zizecology1.htm. Accessed 2015/07/15.

Zuckerhut, P. (2011). Feminist anthropological perspectives on violence. In Ennaji, M. and Sadiqi, F. (Eds), *Gender and violence in the Middle East.* New York: Routledge, pp. 13–25.

2 Gender-based violence and digital technologies

Introduction

The choice of social media in this book is the ubiquitous Facebook, although Twitter is also touched on briefly in Chapter 4. This book is contextualised in the old Facebook which has since changed its name to Meta, which is derived from the term "metaverse." How digital media activism will be impacted by the new-look Facebook (Meta) is yet to be known. This chapter will highlight the sociality of social media, the role of small screens, and how their intersection is heightening digital media feminist activism and touching on topical issues such as GBV. This chapter also provides a deep understanding of what social television implies – if anything – for the discussion of important social issues such as violence against women.

Sociality of social media: a discussion of Facebook and Twitter

What we know so far indicates that Facebook joins together at least three levels of *sociality*: cognition (creating multimedia content such as video and publishing it), communication (commenting, "Liking," and "following"), and cooperation (where others create and manipulate and remix the content). In this chapter, the book is more concerned with the communicative level, where it examines what sort of meanings were being communicated, how, and why. Fuchs explains that at this communicative level, a sense of community is created, complete with sustained social interaction and a sense of familiarity. That is, there is a sense of belonging (Fuchs, 2017, p. 45). Indeed, this model of human sociality appears to emphasise that when humans socialise, they inevitably influence one another and change their "knowledge structures" (Fuchs, 2017, p. 45). This is what makes digital media feminist activism central, since it capitalises on knowledge sharing. The sense of community is one of the driving forces of digital media activism, which relies on spreading messages. The presence of the community is thus salient to reading, examining, and understanding the "talk" and discourse in question. To illustrate the crucial factor of community, Jenkins, Ford, and Green (2013) describe social media as "spreadable media." These authors contend that "if it doesn't spread it's dead" (Jenkins et al., 2013, p. 1). Digital media feminist activism depends on this concept of "spreadable media." This is possible if we consider that by 2022, Facebook had a user base of 2.89 billion people (Wise, 2022). Data shows that at least 25 million South Africans out of a population of about 60 million used social media in 2021.

Social media may not be to everyone's taste, though. A prominent critic, billionaire businessperson George Soros, who spoke at the World Economic Forum (WEF) in January 2018, disputed that social media does us any good.[1] Rather, he regarded Facebook as a sinister online gambling den. His view was that forms of social media are agents of mind control, which seek to influence our behaviour for the ulterior motives of corporations. One way of examining the nature of this influence is through social media "talk," a core focus of this book. What Soros says, if turned around, benefits digital media activism, which seeks to influence behaviour change against malpractices such as GBV.

Despite the negative perceptions of social media, conversations continue with many topics of discussion on social media triggered by what goes on elsewhere, often offline, thus generating trends. One trigger of social media discussion, for instance, is old media, such as television. Most television programmes now have a social media presence in the form of a Twitter handle, a Facebook and Instagram page, and so on, to allow audiences to "Like," "love," "upvote," and "follow" them. Indeed, some scholars of television, such as Wohn and Kyung Na (2011), have started to argue that *the television medium* is no longer what we know it to be at all, where the family would converge as a unit in a room to watch programmes and shows. Rather, a lot of this integrated family television viewing seems to have been interminably *fragmented* into many channels offering specialised niche viewing and, in the age of social media and *interactivity*, seems to have been *overlaid* (some would say *replaced*) by what is known as *social television* (Cesar and Geerts, 2011; Owen, 1999), which is a big influence on digital media activism as it pushes conversations to multi-media platforms. Facebook's Mark Zuckerberg has commented that "We exist at the *intersection* of technology and social issues" (Lee, 2011, p. xiii). This notion of *intersection* of technology and sociality, in as far as it has theoretical validity, aptly captures the spirit of the book.

The Gloria/Obakeng gender violence episodes of the soap opera *Scandal!* are chosen here precisely because, as Gqola (2015, p. 154) posits, "Examples illustrate best, they can work as evidence." Essentially, we turn to examples "for recognition and illumination." The selected episodes of *Scandal!* function as an instrumental case study, opening the way to the broader discussion of attitudes towards, and meaning making about, intimate partner violence. The book thus examines, on the one hand *how* people "talk" about important social issues such as gender violence on social media, why they "talk" this way, and the implications of this "talk" for understanding social relations, and on the other hand, the three-way convergence of "old" media, "new" media, and social forms of "talk." This is important because society is still struggling with the implications of the "network society" (Castells, 2009, p. 5) and is still trying to make sense of what is *really* going on. The proliferation of social media such as Facebook, Twitter, WhatsApp, and Instagram add a further layer of complexity onto the already complex network society. As we saw in the Soros and Wylie examples, there is already an active and polarising debate going on about what is *really* going on in the worlds of social media. This book is a contribution to that question. This question makes this book stand out if we consider that representation of partner violence is not done in a comprehensive manner despite the fact that South Africa has one of the highest rates of intimate partner violence in the world (Isaacs, 2014). What role does social media play in this scourge, and what is *social* about social media and the impact it has on digital media feminist activism?

The word "social" suggests connectedness, and "media" implies platforms. The ubiquitous "Facebook status" tool poses the question to users: "What is on your mind?" On the one hand, statuses are how news spreads quickly through Facebook. Because your posts go into your friends' Live Feeds, a single update can have a big impact and is somewhat likely to be repeated in some way or another (Abraham and Pearlman, 2010, pp. 88–89). On the other hand, the question "What's on your mind?" is tapping the deepest recesses and most private spaces of a person's consciousness. This assumption has been important in formulating the rationale for the study that informed this book. I assumed that, prompted by the Gloria/Obakeng episodes, users would have *a way of "talking"* about what is on their minds about gender violence. Hence the title of this book: *Gender-Based Violence and Digital Media in South Africa*. However, statuses would not have a meaning without the concept of "friends."

Some researchers have made interesting observations regarding the concept of "friends" to describe the people who connect with each other on Facebook. Baym (2012) conducted research to highlight the blurred boundaries between friends and fans. She notes that people called "friends" online may be anything from "strangers to acquaintances, to lovers to family to best friends and more" (Baym, 2012, p. 290). The word "friends" has a standardised definition: "a social, mutually agreed upon connection between two individuals" (Baym, 2012, p. 312). Before Facebook, such a standard definition of friends would not be possible; it would require explicit definitions. In this book, the definition of friends covers fans for the simple reason that Facebook has a limit of 500 friends. To accommodate more than 500 friends, Facebook created fan pages. We will discuss fandom later in this chapter. Measuring social contacts in the real world would be a "tedious task" or "impossible" (Baym, 2012, p. 300). During the pre-social media era, announcing a message to all your friends as we see in Facebook posts was not possible. This Facebook friendship concept is vital for digital media feminist activism to work. Baym (2012, p. 290) contends that experiences such as those offered by Facebook cannot occur anywhere else.

But just who was part of this "talk"? Are they fans or audiences? The answer is both of those. *Scandal!*'s Facebook page was created in 2005. By November 2016 it had garnered 814,054 Facebook "Likes" and over 4000 subscribers. By January 2019 this figure had gone up to 883,194 "Likes," and by May 2022 it had surpassed a million views, as illustrated in Figure 2.1.

This figure increased to 1,078,891 followers by April 2022. Every weekday, *Scandal!*'s producers[2] summarise the previous show in a Facebook post. Fans, including individuals and organisations, log onto the page to "Like," share, or comment about the post. Some comments also get commented on by other fans. Occasionally, fans also post images. Fans can also search for posts on this page or invite friends to "Like" the page. The page also displays video highlights of previous shows, including showing the previous night's full programme. It exhibits photos and gives information about events such as weddings taking place in the programme, announcements of achievements, and competitions. It also offers livestreaming.

Scandal! positions Facebook fans as "barometers" that help to gauge the authenticity of characters, such as do they relate with the audiences or are they in opposition to the character they love? Fans care about the story you tell (Mahlaba, 2023). This perhaps explains why Facebook fan pages help to "develop a deep understanding of the state of mind and attitude of your

Figure 2.1 etvScandal Facebook followers

audience" (Aaker et al., 2010, p. 87) and help to build opportunities for conversations and feedback. Paltoglou (2014, p. 8) calls it "mining opinion." At the same time, not everyone who is part of the online audience is a dedicated fan. Rather, some are anti-fans and trolls who take advantage of the anonymity the internet provides to vent and take conversations off topic. This shows on *Scandal!*'s page, where not every conversation keeps to the script the producers would prefer. Still, the openness of the internet allows fans, anti-fans, and trolls alike to express themselves.

When fans "get involved" and "talk" about the past episodes on domestic violence on *Scandal!*, Jenkins (1992, p. 98) describes this type of "talk" as "meta text." Jenkins views the "talk" as an evaluation of the shows the audience are watching. According to Fiske (1987, p. 78), meta texts are meanings based on what resonates with the cultural needs of that "talking" community. It is what differentiates the audience that just watches television from fans. Fans have knowledge of "interpretive conventions and collaborative metatext used to read the show" (Jenkins, 1992, p. 278). In contemporary times, fans attempt to integrate media representations into their own social experience (Baym, 2000, p. 17), which is what we see with audiences on Twitter's hashtag #AmINext. They offer their own interpretations and evaluations, and set their own cultural canons. Jenkins notes that they blur boundaries between fact and fiction. How feminists are using these platforms to create their own trajectories on issues that affect them becomes critically fundamental, which is why the next chapter will take us to the discussion of the broader feminist politics which the wave of digital media feminist activism discussed in this book is part of.

Fans are audiences. Audiences make media, otherwise the messages that digital media produces would be empty and meaningless. Soap operas and digital media platforms would mean very little without viewers' active participation. It is particularly important to examine the role of audiences, because media functions to shape public opinion and can also exert positive or negative influences (Gunter, 2000). The rise of internet technologies has renewed scrutiny and a close attention to the agency and reflexivity of the people we call "the audience." In the era of social television, the term "audiences" is no longer normatively definable, particularly where new media technologies render audiences indistinguishable, fragmented, dispersed, and invisible (Couldry et al., 2007, p. 157). Yet audiences are real and human, with feelings, thoughts, agency, and subjectivity, even when they are fragmented and dispersed. Ang (1996) forewarned that actual television audiences are inherently unstable and therefore not absolute or definitive, and indeed, declared that there was nothing called the "television audience." Ang correctly predicted at the time that the rise of new television-related technologies would provide people with new options and choices (Ang, 1991, p. 55). Writing in the 1990s, the period when early forms of social media were emerging, Ang (1991, p. 1) expressed concern that television viewer audiences were often ignored. She claimed audiences were "often spoken for or about from a position of distance – by critics, scientists, journalists, teachers, politicians, law makers, advertisers, television producers." But the advent of new media has seen new forms of audiences and audience behaviour emerging. They are more interactive and searching, rather than watching and listening (McQuail, 2010, p. 398). Seen in the light of activism, these audiences drive the point home to men that GBV is wrong. However, if one considers the #AmINext hashtag, the audiences are the media activists who make comments. The book analyses these comments from a feminist perspective. It is activism that has social impact because it may lead to other offline actions such as protests and law reforms, as we will discuss in Chapter 4.

It is now common for soap opera producers to create Facebook fan pages and presences on other social media platforms such as Twitter to encourage television viewers to continue conversations about their favourite programmes there, and to access updates. The word "fan," an abbreviation of the word "fanatic," has its roots in the Latin word *fanaticus* (Jenkins, 1992, p. 12). Fandom, described as a "base for consumer activists who speak back," and who are "assertive" and "opinionated" about their favourite programmes (Jenkins, 2005, p. 284), is the reason the soap opera industry professionals "strive to create a moral text that educates and enlightens as it entertains the audiences" (Blumenthal, 1997, p. 111). Fandom is cultivated or encouraged by broadcasters to build stronger ties with performers and products (McQuail, 2010, p. 442). Ross (2008, p. 3) contends that fandom is what drives television viewers to social media as they seek to share their experiences and be validated. Fans, of course, are also consumers (and products) who make money for those they follow. Both *Scandal!* and Facebook are in business primarily to make money.

Everything that happens on Facebook is exclusive to that digital environment, and these experiences are relevant to real life, and the reality that is mirrored by fans on small screens is illuminated on social media. What, then, is the role of small screens that can help us understand this book further?

Role of small screens

Television programmes trigger conversations and help set the agenda for people's concerns (Livingstone and Hunt, 2001, p. 6; Allen, 2004, p. 1). These kinds of conversations are key to digital media activism as they encourage people to discuss topics that are normally ignored or taboo. This is why we need to understand the questions surrounding the ontology of television, which remains varied and complex (Evans, 2011, p. 17). The ways we have understood television when it was invented in the 1930s and after the advent of social television from 2012 are obviously different. When television was introduced, it was assumed that it would bring families together and help keep marriages alive (Bogart, 1956). As television sets became more affordable to many people, however, television viewing became increasingly individualised. Television birthed the concept of "prime time," which is instrumental in getting messages heard and was the reason the producers of *Scandal!* chose that time for its viewers to watch the GBV episodes. Prime time is defined as the time when the whole family usually watches television (Ang, 1985, p. 56). Prime time is 17:30–22:30 Central African Time. Soap operas are slotted within this prime time as they attract a broad mass audience (Tunstall, 2003, p. 116). Broadcasters capitalise on soap operas to draw in advertisers, where the bulk of the revenue that sustains them is derived. Prime time television has often been used by producers of social change campaigns as a vehicle to drive social discourse and behaviour change, as we see in the Gloria/Obakeng GBV storyline. Johnson (2001) argues that television has "modernising" influences on society, which is true if we look at what has been happening with the #MeToo and #BlackLivesMatter movements. The literature supports the idea that prime television can play a role in preventing domestic violence in the home because it can affect behavioural change (Rushton, 1982). Prime time television such as *Scandal!* can expose social ills such as domestic violence, or at least drive conversation on hot topic issues. Prime time television creates an opportunity for digital media feminist activism to frame issues that affect women and use social media to spread its messages, as *Scandal!* does.

This book is a useful resource despite the important observations about the structural changes brought about by "social television." But what is "social television"? Social television is "the convergence of social media and television." The book thus provides us with a glimpse of what is not known and the actual nature of viewer chat. There are many unknowns – for instance, *how* or *whether* social media has changed the way people "talk" about what they see on television. Further unknowns in this regard concern the content and quality of the discussions on social media threads and what kinds of *knowledge* and *meanings* are being generated on social media threads. The book reveals how *different* or *similar* are these to the kinds of knowledge generated in pre-social media era "talk" and how meanings are generated on social media. Furthermore, the phenomenon of social media chat is unique because it is located on a third-party platform, with its own constraints. The nature of these constraints and how they *alter* communication has not been systematically investigated, and this book provides some knowledge about that. For instance, it helps us understand how social media discussions alter the way discussants read the world and how different social media "talk" is from "talk" in the real world. The book applies and tests all these unknowns by examining how audiences of a local soapie, *Scandal!*, talked about gender violence.

The use of devices now popularly called "second screens" to share viewer experiences through social networking sites is a strategy to increase audience *involvement*. The emergence of social television means the television experience is no longer what it used to be when television was invented nearly a century ago (Brown, 2009, p. 25). For example, people consume content at a rate of 2.5 seconds on television compared with 1.7 seconds on mobile phone (Mazibuko, 2017). In Africa, consumers are known to check their smartphones over several billion times a day, with over one third checking their phones every 5 minutes. Although the proportion of people accessing the internet in Africa is still low (29 per cent) and only 11 per cent are active social media users, the number of active internet users and active social media users had grown by 14 per cent and 25 per cent respectively in 2016, according to Kemp (2016). South Africans spend an average of 7 hours and 2 minutes a day consuming video content and broadcast television, accounting for 42 per cent of the time people spend in front of a television (TechCentral, 2018). Hundreds of millions of viewers now use smartphones, tablets, and laptops to share their television experience with other viewers on social media such as Twitter and Facebook. Social television has the added importance of increasing the reach of people watching programmes, since there are multiple ways of accessing content other than just the screen in the home. This makes television a much more resilient channel of communication in the digital age. Television combines with social media to become a meeting place and marketplace for ideas and experience-sharing, and a learning platform for topical issues, as well as providing an opportunity to express anger and emotions in a way they may have not experienced before, as *Scandal!* shows. The assumption is that the television experience that is plugged in to social media is more "participatory." Social media gives the audiences an opportunity to "talk" back about what they are watching, but goes further to allow audiences to interact with strangers and friends watching the same shows in different homes or locations via social media. These are all ingredients that make digital media feminist activism possible. The question is: how important are soap operas? The next section provides some insights.

Soap opera fantasy or reality?

Although this book is not about the role of soap opera per se, it examines the convergence of a social issue, a social medium, and a television programme to see what meanings such a cocktail throws up. The book thus intersects "old" media (television, soap opera) and "new" media (social media). The unique way in which it proposes and explores not just the notion of "social media "talk" is prime, but how it illustrates this phenomenon with a close reading of actual audiences of a local soapie and the way it attempts to answer some of the unknowns regarding social television and soap operas. Apparently, soap opera is the most popular genre and crowd puller on South African television after advertisements, news, reality, sports, and music.[3] News trailed in fifth position, with only about 29 per cent of viewership. Compared to other soapies in the country, *Scandal!* is ranked fifth, according to 2018 statistics on the ten most-watched soapies in South Africa, so it is a big player in the social television space (Thelwell, 2014). *Scandal!* is currently watched by 4.8 million

38 GBV and digital technologies

people in South Africa alone, according to etv's prime time 2016 statistics of the station's top 20 programmes watched by viewers from the age group 15 years and above. This is about 40 per cent of etv's viewer share.

Soap operas are considered to carry a message. They "constitute one of the most popular and resilient forms of storytelling ever devised" (Allen, 2001, p. 1). In 1920, when soap operas were introduced, they were mainly sponsored by soap manufacturers targeting stay-at-home spouses. Although soap operas are still overwhelmingly targeting women, they are no longer simply viewed as some form of "trash" by critics. Soap operas now provide entertainment to a broad-based mass audience of both men and women (Ang, 1985, p. 56). The growth of soap operas is the reason why the genre has increasingly been used since the 1980s to address social issues and scholars have taken a serious interest in soapies in their studies (Geraghty, 2001, p. 76). The soap operas' association with the audience, which broadcasters perceive as a source of potential revenue through advertisements, is also what makes the genre popular (Ang, 1991, p. 4). There is obviously a strong link between soap operas and television.

Allen (2001, p. 4) argues that soap operas, like digital media, are about exposing "dirt" because they deal with secrets such as extramarital liaisons, mistaken marriages, and children given up for adoption. Indeed, *Scandal!*'s Facebook page confirms this mechanism: "*Scandal* has it all: provocative plots; conflict, confrontation and crisis; intrigue; family feuds; true love; shock surprises and shameful secrets; handsome men and beautiful women; villains, heroes and heroines; crime; coups and hidden agendas." Soaps themselves are set in places which maximise interaction and conflict, where characters congregate, such as in the media, hospitals, law firms, police stations, and places of entertainment. Episodes aim to keep storylines current and interesting and introduce plotlines which are controversial, social, and moral. The *Scandal!* episodes mirror real-life murders of women like those discussed by #AmINext Twitter audiences. The #AmINext hashtag thus resembles a never-ending real-life soap opera characterised by the alarming GBV statistics in South Africa covered in Chapter 1. As Hobson (2003, p. 116) states, soap operas are about the family, or life within or between families, and this is true for *Scandal!* Soap operas' ability to combine content that is controversial with carrying powerful storylines that provoke debate is the reason they are used to campaign against social ills in society. They take on difficult issues, and in the case of *Scandal!*, are used as a channel and platform to dramatise the social dilemmas of domestic violence. Fans turn to *Scandal!*'s Facebook pages to express their opinions about the soap opera's episodes on domestic violence.

Soap opera industry professionals "strive to create a moral text that will educate and enlighten as it entertains the audiences" (Blumenthal, 1997, p. 111). Soap opera was thus the "hook," the trigger, for the "talk" that manifests itself as digital media activism that characterises this book. "Talk," in this context, is not cheap. The soapie provided the story and plotlines on the issue of intimate partner violence which was described in Chapter 1. Social media was the field in which raw data was mined, as has already been mentioned. This signifies that people "are living life online," and, for many, "life online is as real as life offline" (Lee, 2011, p. 150). This was very much the case with both the *Scandal!* and #AmINext audiences. *Scandal!* confirmed that audiences are still very much eager to watch soap operas and "talk" about them with family and friends, as Baym (2000, p. 14) also discovered. According to Brown (2009, p. 18), it appears that people go onto social media sites partly for FOMO (fear of missing out), but also to experience a separate online identity that is somehow an extension and a mirror of the offline one. The soap opera genre, on the other hand, gives viewers something to *"talk" about* because of the way it is structured – for instance, it stitches audiences into "endless narratives," as Brunsdon (2000, p. 173) observes.

In South Africa, soap operas were introduced to television in the 1990s and were mostly exclusively for white female audiences, focusing on "feminine interests" such as family and romantic love (Burton, 2012, p. 222). Burton speculates that the soap operas were not introduced earlier because the Apartheid regime could not "fathom how a woman centred genre could further the aims of its apartheid-era social and economic policies." Advertisers targeted women with products such as shampoos, adverts showcasing product ranges at retail chain stores, and time-specific commercials such as Mother's Day (Burton, 2012, p. 222). Focusing on stay-at-home spouses and desires of white women was meant to promote dominant ideologies about race. All this changed with the coming of the democratic South Africa in 1994. Soap operas were beginning to be modelled around "Africanness" to promote African identity and change the way Africans are perceived and represented in the media (Burton, 2012, p. 224). Hence this book adopts a hybrid feminism approach including Black feminism, as we shall explore in detail in the next chapter.

Although early research on daytime serials criticised them for being "immoral," "unhealthy," and causing "anxiety" in viewers (Allen, 1985, pp. 21–22; Buckman, 1985, p. 163), feminist epistemology on soap opera has helped to change people's perceptions about the genre, awakening many to the reality that soap opera is not frivolous women's gossip, but a complex, layered, and meaningful genre that appeals to a variety of audiences (Baym, 2000, p. 4). *Scandal!'s* Facebook page claims that *Scandal!* "always reflects the realities of life in South Africa," and this is aptly demonstrated by #AmINext Twitter audiences who talk about real murders of women in the country, and this point will be expounded in Chapter 4. *Scandal!*, although sounding like an exaggeration, accords well with the view that soap operas are not mere gossip, but rather, also concern themselves with complex and serious themes. The page goes on to claim that *Scandal!* does not shy away from controversial issues: alcoholism, drug addiction, and depression – and the recovery processes; HIV and anti-retroviral drugs, sexual abuse, sweatshops, political activism, and looking behind the scenes of investigative journalism, bringing up the point on representation. One cannot fully fathom feminism without examining representation, and this is explained in the next chapter. Geraghty (2001, p. 76) addresses the representation of women in soap operas, the pleasures and values offered to them, and the nature of themes, topics, and issues the soap operas cover, and helps us realise how soap opera is viewed in some quarters as a feminist genre because of its historic links with women. It is no wonder *Scandal!'s* GBV episodes spill over to social media. Brundson (2000, p. 173), one of the early scholars to view soap operas from a feminist perspective, examined how female viewers read or enjoyed soap operas. Brundson's work reveals that television watching is a cultural contestation that involves the active production of meaning by viewers (Ang, 1996, p. 26), and these days digital media extends this "talk" to online spaces. Viewers see soap opera characters as true to life and living in situations like their own (Spence, 2001, p. 188), hence they can relate to them and take the conversations online. Viewers find television soap operas compelling because they believe they are getting to know about people and life although they are clearly constructs. Blumenthal found soap operas to fundamentally offer a "relaxing space" for women, and now, coupled with digital media, these messages spread and allow others to join in the conversation. This book, however, is not necessarily preoccupied with how women are represented per se, but how soap opera as a representational system sparks social discourse and offers a gateway to insights about social change.

Notes

1 Soros, G. (25 January 2018). "Remarks delivered at the World Economic Forum", https://www.georgesoros.com/2018/01/25/remarks-delivered-at-the-world-economic-forum/. Accessed 6 March 2018.
2 etvScandal Facebook page, https://www.facebook.com/etvScandal/.
3 Thelwell, E. (22 August 2014). "7 things you should absolutely know about TV soapies". news24, https://www.news24.com/life/7-things-you-should-absolutely-know-about-tv-soapies-20140822 Accessed 27 November 2016.

References

Aaker, J., Smith, A., & Adler, C. (2010). *The dragon fly effect: Quick, effective and powerful ways to use social media, to driver social change*. Stanford, CA: Jossey-Bass.

Allen, R.C. (1985). *Speaking of soap operas*. Chapel Hill, NC: University of North Carolina Press.

Allen, R.C. (2001). Introduction. In Allen, R.C. (Ed), *To be continued …soap operas around the world*. London: Routledge, pp. 1–26.

Allen, R.C. (2004). Introduction. In Allen, R.C., & Hill, A. (Eds), *The television studies reader*. London: Routledge, pp. 1–26.

Ang, I. (1985). *Watching Dallas. Soap opera and the melodramatic imagination*. London: Methuen.

Ang, I. (1991). *Desperately seeking the audience*. London: Routledge.

Ang, I. (1996). *Living room wars: Rethinking media audiences for a post-modern world.* London: Routledge.
Baym, N.K. (2000). *Tune in, log on: Soaps, fandom, and online community.* London: Sage Publications.
Baym, N.K. (2012). Fans or friends? Seeing social media audiences as musicians do participations. *Journal of Audience and Reception Studies,* 9(2), 286–316.
Blumenthal, D. (1997). *Women and soap opera: A cultural feminist perspective.* London: Praeger Publishers.
Brunsdon, C. (2000). *The feminist, the housewife and the soap opera.* Oxford: Clarendon press.
Brown, R. (2009). *Public relations and the social web: How to use social media and web 2.0 in communications.* London: Replika press.
Bogart, L. (1956). *The age of television: A study of viewing habits and the impact of television on American life.* New York: F. Ungar.
Buckman, P. (1985). *All for love: A study in soap opera.* Salem: N H. Merrimack.
Burton, N. (2012). South African soapies: A "rainbow nation" realised? In Smith-Shomade, B.E. (Ed), *Watching while black: Centering the television of black audiences.* London: Rutgers University Press, pp. 220–231.
Castells, M. (2009). *Communication power.* Oxford: Oxford University Press.
Cesar, P., & Geerts, D. (2011). Past, present, and future of social TV: A categorisation. 3rd IEEE International workshop on social TV- the Nest Wave.
Couldry, N., Livingstone, H., & Markham, T. (Eds). (2007). *Media consumption and public engagement: Beyond the presumption of attention.* New York: Palgrave Macmillan.
Evans, E. (2011). *Transmedia television: Audiences, new media, and daily life.* London: Routledge.
Fiske, J. (1987). *Television culture.* London: Routledge.
Fuchs, C. (2017). *Social media: A critical introduction* (Second Edition). London: Sage.
Gqola, D.P. (2015). *Rape: A South African nightmare.* Johannesburg: JM Books.
Geraghty, C. (2001). Social issues and realist soaps. A study of British soaps in the 1980/1990s. In Allen, R.C. (Ed), *To be continued...Soaps around the world.* London: Routledge, pp. 66–80.
Gunter, B. (2000). *Media research methods: Measuring audiences, reactions, and impact.* London: Sage Publications.
Hobson, D. (2003). *Soap opera.* Cambridge: Polity.
Isaacs, D.H. (2014). Social representations of intimate partner violence in the South African media. *South African Journal of Psychology,* 46(4), 491–503.
Jenkins, H. (1992). *Textual poachers: Television fans and participatory culture.* London: Routledge.
Jenkins, H. (2005). Buy these problems because they're fun to solve: A conversation with Will Wright. *Telemedium: The Journal of Media Literacy,* 52(1&2), 20–23.
Jenkins, H., Ford, S., & Green, J. (2013). *Spreadable media: Creating value and meaning in a networked culture.* New York: New York University Press.
Johnson, K. (2001). Media and social change: The modernising influences of TV in rural India. *Media, Culture and Society,* 23(2), 147–160.
Kemp, S. (2016). 2016 Digital yearbook. We are social's compendium of key digital statistics and data points for 232 countries around the world. https://www.mom-gmr.org/uploads/tx_lfrogmom/documents/3-167_import.pdf Accessed 2019/03/01.

Lee, N. (2011). *Facebook nation: Total information awareness*. New York: Springer.
Livingstone, S., & Lunt, P. (2001). *Talk on television: Audience participation and public debate*. London: Routledge.
Mahlaba, G. (2023). WhatsApp interview. Johannesburg. 14 February. Interview notes available from the author.
Mazibuko, S. (2017). Sifiso Mazibuko speaking on the art and science of FB marketing at Meltwater. Home page. https://www.facebook.com/networkexplosion/videos/1453356891424535/. Accessed 2017/05/31.
McQuail, D. (2010). *McQuail's mass communication theory*. London: Sage.
Owen, B.M. (1999). *The internet challenge to television*. Cambridge, MA: Harvard University Press.
Paltoglou, G. (2014). Sentiment analysis in social media. In Wig, R.T., Lim, M., & Agarwal, N. (Eds), *Online collective action: Dynamics of the crowd in social media*, London: Springer, pp. 3–18.
Pearlman, L., & Abram, C. (2010). *Facebook® for dummies®*. Toronto: John Wiley & Sons.
Ross, S.M. (2008). *Beyond the box: Television and the Internet*. Oxford: Blackwell Publishing.
Rushton, J.P. (1982). Television and prosocial behaviour. In Pearl, D., Bouthilet, L., & Lazar, J. (Eds), *Television and behaviour*, Volume 2 Technical review. Washington, DC: National Institute of Mental Health, pp. 248–257.
Spence, L. (2001). "They killed off Marlena, but she's on another show now": Fantasy, reality, and pleasure in watching daytime soap operas. In Allen, R.C. (Ed), *To be continued …soap operas around the world*. London: Routledge, pp. 182–198.
Techcentral. (2018). Urban SA turning its back on linear pay TV, GfK says. Home page. https://www.techcentral.co.za/south-africans-turning-their-backs-on-linear-pay-tv/80979/. Accessed 2018/05/22.
Thelwell, E. (2014). 7 things you should absolutely know about TV soapies. Home page. http://www.channel24.co.za/TV/News/7-things-you-should-absolutely-know-about-TV-soapies-20140822. Accessed 2016/11/27.
Tunstall, J. (2003). *Television producers*. London: Routledge.
Wise, J. (2022). Social media usage statistics 2022: Demographics, trends and countries. Home page. https://earthweb.com/social-media-usage-statistics/. Accessed 2021/05/02.
Wohn, D.Y., & Kyung-Na, E. (2011). Tweeting about TV: Sharing television viewing experiences via social media message streams. *First Monday*, 16(3). Home page. https://firstmonday.org/ojs/index.php/fm/article/view/3368/2779 Accessed 2020/06/10.

3 African feminist ideology politics and gender-based violence

Introduction

The feminist theory framework used in this book serves as a model of social justice whose core function helps us to see that women are full human beings who are not made in the image of patriarchy. Although *Scandal!* acknowledges that Gloria is a feminist representation, it did not have feminism in mind when it conceptualised the Gloria/Obakeng GBV storyline (Mahlaba, 2023). This is because its township audience would not know that word. The hardships, including GBV, that the township women experience daily are viewed as survival, and as we will discuss later, many practise feminism without knowing the word. *Scandal!* wanted Black women to be heard, and the episodes served as a helpline. For example, women needed to realise that you cannot be stuck with in-laws and that violence can happen to the woman next door. The intention was to show that no matter how upright a person is, they may not see violence coming and there is no room for judging people. The producers wanted to show audiences that once they recognise GBV, they must speak up. People had to be aware of it.

Feminism is thus utilised in this book as a reminder that women as a group are misrepresented – in both the public sphere and in the conception of their real natures (Pilcher and Whelehan, 2004, pp. xii–xiii). It was also as a reminder that women's local knowledge is often overlooked. Feminism is not static, and digital media feminist activism is an example of how feminist politics has evolved. The theory is used in this book as an analytical framework, without which it will be impossible to make sense of the various forms of GBV, how it affects women, and manifests.

In the past, there was a demand for voices that took leadership and spoke out on women's oppression, such as bell hooks, Patricia Hill Collins, Dineo Gqola, Ifi Amadiume, and Glenda Daniels, to name a few African feminists. With today's technology wave, the echoes of women of all backgrounds, races, and classes resound in different directions, in a way that means it is not easy to identify any one voice as a leadership voice for women. Defining feminism has proven to be anything but simple (Mekgwe, 2008). At the outset, it is worth pointing out that feminism as a political ideology never stays the same, but is always changing and finding new and

DOI: 10.4324/9781003260820-3

better avenues to utilise and explore using methodologies that are feminist-centred (Mikell, 1997).

This book uses a blended feminist theory to analyse the core subject of digital media feminism. Blending feminist theory leads us into uncharted territory (Defrancisco, 1997). A blended theoretical positioning was fundamental for this book because the social media that shapes this book is relatively new. The diversity of discourses and positions that arise in social media "talk" about intimate partner violence are important to know and understand from various angles. All feminists share a basic commitment to ending female oppression of women, but no doubt do not approach the problem in the same way, even if gender, knowledge, and power are always *interrelated*. What this chapter will do, therefore, is to describe the various framing elements of Black feminist online "anthropology," which scholars such a McLaurin (2001) describe as a conscious act of knowledge production and canon formation. All the theories combined in this chapter are merely an entry point to reflecting on and constructing theory, praxis, politics, and poetics of social media chat on gender violence. As South Africa continues to top international rankings for the incidence of gender violence, this book is an intervention. It is part of what Britton (2006) calls "organising against gender violence in South Africa."

The chapter thus evaluates how meaning about women and women's issues (in this case, gender violence) is constructed in the social media context and how such a construction responds to shifting perceptions of women and femininity. Feminist movements are credited for putting women's issues on the agenda. Feminism, as an activist movement and as a body of ideas, underlines the need for a positive transformation of society such that women are not marginalised, but are treated as full citizens in all spheres of life (Mekgwe, 2008, p. 16). The women's movement was the driving force behind the wider feminist politics, and has been instrumental in making violence against women recognised as a human right. However, the struggle is far from over, and the visibility cannot be taken for granted, as South Africa's statistics on GBV show. There is a perception you cannot continue to challenge patriarchy within social movements of the past. As hooks (2000, p. xiv) points out, the feminist movement has not yet created a sustained feminist revolution because of the systemic incidence of patriarchy, sexism, and oppression, but digital media feminist activism seems to be challenging this perception, as we have witnessed with the #MeToo and #BlackLivesMatter movements. In fact, the global women's movement as we knew it is dead, although new forms of feminisms are springing up. The main danger, as hooks notes, is that any feminist gains are always at risk of being undone, but time will tell how digital media feminist activism will turn out.

It also needs to be pointed out at the outset that there is a general suspicion of feminism among African women, Indigenous women, and women of colour, such as Amadiume (1997), Oyewumi (2005), Hill Collins (2004),

Geisler (2004), and hooks (1982) because the concept is, on the one hand, regarded as being a Western import that perpetuates whiteness, and on the other hand, because of the invisibility of the oppressed of the non-Western world. Digital media feminist activism is showing us that feminism is no longer about women, but people in general, and particularly that gender lines are no longer drawn around "he" or "she," but there is now a whole range of identity preferences coming into play. Some people do not identify themselves as women or men, but as "they" or "it." Feminism is almost syncretic, where it is mixed with other ideas, and thus it is no longer prominent, with some believing feminism is dead. Those who believe that feminism is extinct pay little attention to traditional feminism that focuses on women, but rather are more concerned with violation of rights in general, which may include feminism. To them, GBV is where one of those rights is often violated. They also pay less attention to patriarchy and masculinity, believing that the justice system must have power over any injustice, including GBV. Some believe that feminism alone without carrying the ideas of men is not enough, as we will explore later.

The concept of feminism has also been castigated for losing sight of the interests of "ordinary" women like Gloria, an ordinary Black African woman who works as an office cleaner. Davis and Tadia (2005, p. 3) observe that the designation "women of colour" is a political category emerging out of US-based struggles. As such, it cannot be expected to travel easily beyond the national boundaries of the US without contradictions or tensions. Nevertheless, the term has its uses, particularly in enabling "a political coalition of diverse, particular histories of struggle" of "Native American, Chicana/o, African American, Hawaiian, Asian American, as well as immigrant Third World women struggles." At any rate, South Africa, newly emerging out of Apartheid, is as heavily racialised as the US. Gloria's body exists within similar frames of racial politics to those that face "women of colour" in the US and elsewhere. Black feminism thus places Black women and their experiences at the centre of analysis. For Black feminists, the dominant conception of feminism reflects white values and experiences and fails to consider how Black women see the world. Western feminist theory presents itself as a universal phenomenon, doing so in ways which disguise its profoundly Western concerns and biases (Mohanty, Russo, and Torres, 1991, p. 53). As Hill Collins points out in *Black Sexual Politics* (2004, p. 2), "gender, age, social class, and education do not matter if you are Black." There are differences in penalty and privilege that accompany race, class, and similar systems of social injustice. Furthermore, it is not enough to imagine empowerment for Black women in isolation from deep-seated changes in the overall social structure (Hill Collins, 2004). Comments about Gloria were scrutinised from two viewpoints: for how they read her race as well as her class. This book avoids what Patricia Hill Collins regards as the narrowness of the white feminist analysis (Hill Collins, 1990, p. 119). Even if we suppose that each

Black woman has a common, shared struggle, the form it takes differs greatly, as well as our responses to it.

Postmodern feminism was also used as a model to form this book because this kind of feminism tends to be more comfortable with plurality and multiple truths. Postmodern feminism in general opens the book to a rich polysemy of ideas about women, the invisibility of power, the mediation of technology, and femininity. As the world transitions from modernity, there is no one single hegemonic truth, but rather multiple realities (East, 1998). In the past, construction of new family or marital laws was more of a reactionary response to socio-economic trauma affecting women and children, but these days women are more proactive in resisting hegemonic policies that hinder women's progress and pushing for changes (Mikell, 1997).

Cyberfeminism, for its part, is considered an analytical tool in this book because it seeks to evaluate modes and spaces of social media "talk" which sometimes alienate women. Chatting on social media is an instance of cyberculture. In Africa, this may be hampered by lack of internet infrastructure, high data costs, and the expense of smartphones. The interest in this book goes further than just an interest in the cyberculture of social media "talk," to explore the dynamics of such online interaction in relation to intimate partner violence. This aspect is perhaps reflected not so much by gender affiliation, but by the feminist ideas of participants. This is because cyberfeminism expresses the hybrid relationship between feminist theory and what is known as cyberculture, and is more concerned with how people, including women, are using the digital space. Cyberfeminism is relevant in this book because of its interest in using technology to advance views, perspectives, and experiences of women to combat oppression directed at women.

That said, the book draws on a strand of African feminism that is more organic to Africa. African feminism, broadly, is shaped by African women's resistance to Western hegemony. This cocktail of theories speaks to representation and online identity issues which we will discuss next before expounding on the various feminisms this book utilises.

What's GBV got to do with representation and online identity?

This book was curated in the context of representation and online identity. This is because the online world has been identified as a contradictory and ambivalent space in which the representation and perception of gender is fluid, and the book provides evidence that such fluidity may be positive or negative. At the same time, the ability to create multiple and fragmented identities is, for some, liberating. It touches on issues of masculinity and patriarchy, given how these are central in feminist discourse.

Representation is important in this book because the central text that sparked the social media "talk" that is analysed in this book consists of episodes drawn from a popular South African television soap opera, *Scandal!* How the episodes of intimate partner violence between Gloria and Obakeng were represented is central to how they were talked about on social media. Several books have looked at the convergence of feminism and representation in general and with such "feminine" genres as soap opera. This one differs not only for its focus on the changing technology landscape that has brought in more new concepts that were not there before, such as social television and its intersection with the proliferation of small screens, but also because it brings perspectives of GBV among Black marginalised women. The *Scandal!* and #AmINext case studies in this book mirror how most South African Black women are struggling under GBV.

Representation

Representation is a complex topic. Blumenthal (1997) equates soap operas to illustration of women's culture. Afro-feminist Tsitsi Dangarembga awakens us to the point that media represents a social voice and position of authority, so when women's issues are made public, it is social empowerment, and when they are not, it is a social disadvantage. By concentrating on the topic of domestic violence, *Scandal!* was attempting to mirror reality and shape audiences' understanding of reality, and #AmINext was a confirmation of those realities where Black women are daily living with GBV in South Africa. This representation was made more alive because television acts as a type of a mirror for reality (Baudrillard, 1991). Fourie (2008, p. 260), however, argues that the media, like other symbolic systems, "are not simple reflections of some external, grounded truth." Fourie calls media representations a "mediated version" of reality because he argues that a television news programme "can never offer the whole of the reality" (Fourie, 2008, p. 199). While Fourie's observations are true, representations on social media, unlike television, are more real as people often articulate their own lived experiences if they are not trolls or bots. Although critics have traditionally faulted soaps "for their lack of social realism" (Modleski, 1979, p. 16), the same cannot be said of the selected episodes from *Scandal!* The subject of intimate partner violence ensures that these episodes contain more than enough social realism. We see Gloria going through psychological abuse as she tries to please her victimiser, without success. For instance, she gets Obakeng a birthday present, which he rejects. She then tries to throw him a surprise birthday party, but he is unhappy with her effort. As he grows tired of Gloria, he becomes constantly critical of her, her habits, and her friends. He habitually and constantly lashes out at her. This abuse is consistent with the cycle of GBV described in Chapter 1.

The subject of violence against women is both a representational and theoretical issue in this book. There is an assumption by the producers of *Scandal!* that there is a one-to-one correspondence between the representation and reality. For instance, violence against Gloria represented all women living with this type of abuse. In terms of the 16 Days of Activism theme, Obakeng's character is an epitome of an abusive man, while Gloria, whom he abuses, represents the almost one in three women in South Africa who face violence from their intimate partners. This kind of representation where GBV is being talked about through fan social media outlets like etvScandal and the #AmINext hashtag is part of online identity culture-forming.

Online identity

The act of posting comments and views online, such as on the etvScandal Facebook page and the #AmINext hashtag, which will be discussed in the next chapter, is a process of creating an online identity (Baym, 2000; Howarth, 2011). Baym (2000) calls it a form of representing the self. This form of representation is a point of focus in the book, particularly in terms of how this online identity frames women in the discussion of GBV. The media, whether old or new, plays a big role in shaping our lives. The new media has added identities based on online "social" interaction that are not only mass-produced, but are produced by media users themselves through internet social network sites such as Facebook and Twitter (Fourie, 2008, p. 259). In other words, these media outlets are representational systems. Woodward (2002, p. 74) tells us that representational systems help us to "make sense of both ourselves and of others" and are "crucial to the marking of both difference and sameness." This was the case in both the etvScandal and #AmINext social media "talks" that are the subjects of this book, where audiences not only shared their own experiences about GBV, but also shared opinions about what Gloria should do or not do, including comments about the man who abuses Gloria, Obakeng, and calling him names. On the #AmINext hashtag, for example, there is a lot of redefining and questioning of gender, rape, men, and feminism by audience members as they search for meanings about GBV. Soap operas are a form of representation via which viewers participate in identity construction. Social position, background, and cultural orientation are central to identity construction. Fourie (2008) notes that the context in which viewers consume media has an influence on how they construct their identities in relation to media content and is well articulated by Michel Foucault.

Foucault on power

Stuart Hall's and Michel Foucault's theories of the construction of identity illustrate that there is an inextricable relationship between representation and power. The avenue of representation and power is certainly one way of analysing online identity (Fourie, 2008, p. 219). We see the power of the *Scandal!* social media "talk" followers in their rejection of the positioning of Gloria, who is represented as a woman who is indecisive and tolerates abuse by not reporting her abuser to the police or relatives. *Scandal!* points out that it is not an issue if a woman is indecisive, because if she is not yet ready to leave her marriage, she will not do so. Gloria's going back and forth is a normal way of processing violence because it is hard to leave a marriage. When a woman has been humiliated enough and she wants to stop violence against her and is ready to leave an abusive marriage, she may come out alive or dead. In the case of Gloria, she came out alive. *Scandal!* also wanted to show that regardless of age, women love a "happily ever after ending," so Gloria believed that Obakeng had done her a favour to love her. *Scandal!* also wanted people to move away from the stereotype that regardless of age, a woman can leave a marriage if it does not work out and move on "because we come from a society that says: 'What will people say?'" (Mahlaba, 2023). Followers of the soap opera's social media "talk" argue that this kind of representation of Gloria sends bad signals to other abused women. But Gloria is only mirroring reality, which presents *Scandal!* audience members with an opportunity to seek solutions within themselves. In this case, social media is not just a place to socialise, but it is for self-identification and renewal. In the #AmINext Twitter "talk" discussed in the next chapter, commenters push for change and organise online protests and the signing of petitions demanding that GBV be declared an emergency and that the abolished death penalty in South Africa be reinstated for crimes against women. This is organised feminism, even though it is not explicit.

Foucault's focus on power through language is an important theoretical departure for this book. Sundén (2002, p. 295) reminds us that textual "talk" takes place "in a rarely acknowledged borderland between 'talk' and text" where language becomes the only thing there is. She describes textual "talk" as "texts," composed of written words, based entirely on the activity of reading and writing. In Chapter 5, we will explore how language has helped to transform the discourse about GBV on social media and helps us to form Indigenous feminist knowledge. The use of Indigenous languages and expressions common in sub-Saharan Africa gives GBV in the global South a new kind of nuance and understanding. This is critical because it changes narratives about GBV on social media that are rarely discussed in patriarchal media spaces that are dominated by men.[1] *Scandal!* reckons that language is key, and is always looking at where it can add more languages. Audiences love languages they can speak. South Africa officially has 11 languages. Recent studies on user-generated content such as social media, however, show a vastly different picture: women dominate the use of social networking sites such as Facebook more than men (Wiese et al., 2014, p. 3). There has certainly been a radical shift occasioned by social media.

The book also helps to show insights into the way audiences "talk" about *Scandal!*, without any attempt to profile the gender of participants. Whatever views were obtained from Facebook were subjected to a feminist interpretation. But as Vasilescu, Capiluppi, and Serebrenik (2012) observe, online identity can be impeded by various factors. Users often choose gender-neutral names or opposite-sex avatars and names to negotiate a male-dominated space. The use of gender-neutral names or "male profiles" is an effort to be accepted by the mostly male participants, for fear of misogyny. Gender deception is often the result of cyber harassment, where women will disguise their gender to articulate their views without fear (Choja and Nelson, 2016). Choja and Nelson (2016) found that women are largely victims of cyber harassment. They further point out that women are turned off by the blatant sexism of participants and compelled to leave these online communities. Describing an account of gender swapping, Stone (1995, p. 181) cites a disabled older woman who seemed to have a powerful and enabling effect on the many women who interacted with her on cyberspace. Eventually, she was revealed to be a man, and "her" followers online felt a sense of betrayal. These illustrations suggest that avatars are not self-representations in a constructed online space, and thus are not really "real people." The expectation that gender identity in online space mirrors that in real life becomes blurred. The online world becomes an ambivalent space in which the fluidity of gender may be positive or negative, although others have reported feeling that the ability to create multiple and fragmented identities is liberating (Turkle, 1995, p. 184; Wolmark, 2003).

Arguing that online identities are difficult to define because of the blurred lines between bodies and technology, Turkle (1995, p. 228) suggests that disembodied communication has the potential to free society from discrimination based on race, sex, gender, sexuality, or class. The issue of discrimination brings the question of which feminism is appropriate. The book attempts to answer that by examining what is meant by the term "feminism."

Which feminism?

It is common to hear people rejecting the label "feminist" (Antrobus, 2004, p. 144). Pilcher and Whelehan (2004) assert that the term "feminism" originates from the French word *féminisme*, which was a medical term used in the 19th century to refer to masculine women or men with feminized traits. In the 20th century, the term was used in the United States to refer to a group of women "which asserted the uniqueness of women, the mystical experience of motherhood and women's special purity" (Pilcher and Whelehan, 2004, p. 48). Today, the term, though "overburdened with meaning" (Pilcher and Whelehan, 2004, p. 66), generally means someone who is committed to transforming women's subordinated social position (Mekgwe, 2008). Mekgwe's definition is also as problematic as the term "woman" itself. Certainly, what is meant by masculinity or femininity is the subject of continuing interrogation. This includes critiques of the notion of gender itself. Such critiques are important in this book. The book uses the term "gender" often. Gender does not denote "biological or anatomical differences between men and women" (this would be sex), but is concerned with the psychological, social, and cultural *difference* between male and female (Giddens, 1989, p. 158). As Hill Collins (2004, p. 6) notes, talking about gender does not mean focusing solely on women's issues. Rather, men's experiences are also deeply gendered. Thus, gender ideology not only creates ideas about femininity, but it also shapes conceptions of masculinity. Regardless of race, ethnicity, social class, citizenship status, and sexual orientation, all people encounter social norms about gender. These norms influence people's sense of themselves as people as well as perceptions of masculinity and femininity.

Giddens (1989) argues that it makes no sense to assume that there is merely one set of traits that generally characterises men and thus defines masculinity, or likewise, that there is one set of traits for women which defines femininity. This point is worth noting in this book, which uses a polysemic feminist framework to analyse the digital media activism at the centre of focus. Later, we note that feminism is not an ideology for women only. One cannot assume that because someone is a woman they are automatically a feminist, or that all men are anti-feminist. Essentially, the femininity/masculinity binary is loosened and, indeed, thrown into some confusion. Hill Collins (2004) points out that for Black people, the relationship between gender and race is intensified, producing "a Black gender ideology" that shapes ideas about Black masculinity and Black femininity.

Masculinity is linked to patriarchy, in the sense that men tend to benefit materially and socially from patriarchy. In South Africa, the patriarchal system is embedded in society regardless of race or class (Pillay, 2010.) Dealing with it requires attacking it at its roots. It is in this sense that radical and Marxist feminists have viewed patriarchy as a concrete problem concerning women's general well-being and progress, and we see this in *Scandal!* too, where Gloria is supposed to be a conformist. There is need, for example, for creating spaces for equal gender representation and integrating interventions that transform the lives of women socially, educationally, and economically. We notice, for instance, that when the abuse in *Scandal!* starts, the abuser, Obakeng, criticises Gloria for everything, lashes out at her at every conceivable point, and criticises her friends. Gloria can never do anything right.

Whereas Western patriarchy seeks to control and rule women, this is not the case with *matrifocal* African "patriarchy." Rather, African patriarchy is much more complex and nuanced. Whereas patriarchy, as framed in Western terms, is problematic because it celebrates violence, valour, conquest, and power, and is generally oppressive, African women have not experienced patriarchy in quite this way. African women have had more authority, power, and autonomy (Amadiume, 1997; Geisler, 2004; Mikell, 1997). It is in this sense that Amadiume speaks, for instance, of "male daughters" and "female sons." Black feminists, at any rate, have never regarded as sufficient the analysis of patriarchy in the absence of race and the history of colonialism, empire, and slavery (Pilcher and Whelehan, 2004, p. 96). There is therefore increasingly more inclination towards using "patriarchy" only as an adjective to describe individuals or institutions that exploit women, rather than viewing it as a central concept of gender theory (Pilcher and Whelehan, 2004). Tracing patriarchy or feminism on social media is challenging because it is not possible to determine the gender of those talking. Patriarchy and feminism can be discerned through language and the ideas that emerge from such a "talk."

There is some scope to extend the discussion of how patriarchy is normatively regarded in the West as opposed to the matriarchal tradition in Africa. Much of the scholarship traces the source of virulent masculinity to colonialism (Amadiume, 1997). At least, colonialism is blamed for removing African women from the public domain by, for instance, encouraging men to take over the agricultural production which African women were in control of, and peripheralising women through training them in home crafts (Amadiume, 1997).

In general, research shows that women remain easy targets of violence, exclusion, victimisation, and abuse. Walby (1990) argues that women's household production, paid work, the state, male violence, sexuality, and culture altogether "capture the depth, pervasiveness and interconnectedness of women's subordination." Basically, such gendered violence is often systemic. For instance, it has been suggested that there is a correlation between violence against women and economic deprivation (McFadden, 2007). This is seen where violence against women is prevalent in African countries beset with high unemployment (McFadden, 2007). The loss of African women's economic power and their general economic peripheralisation under colonialism has resulted in acute male domination (Geisler, 2004). Geisler traces the persistence of a strong strain of gender-based violence in Africa to this origin. For this reason, Walby (1990) argues that patriarchy cannot be defeated until systemic oppression of women is ended.

In my reading, it is in the critique of the femininity/masculinity binary that African feminism is strongest. For instance, Amadiume (1997) and Oyewumi (1997) have built a strong scholarship that rejects the traditional binarities between masculine and feminine, and what they see as the deliberate but unacceptable and distorting *masculinisation* of African societies. Oyewumi argues that the Yoruba language is not gendered, and categories such as "male" or "female" do not translate easily into the language (1997, p. 33). The situation of patriarchy as a central concept in feminism theory is problematic because it assumes that patriarchy is universal, overlooking cultural difference. That is, it appears to assume that gender relations between men and women are the same everywhere. Yet patriarchy need not mean the same thing everywhere, for everyone. Pilcher and Whelehan (2004, p. 36) go further to criticise the assumption that gender relations are only between men and women. In fact, gender relations are also between women and women and men and men.

Amadiume and Oyewumi's writings highlight how Western scholarship about Africa in general traditionally tended to ignore the important role played by the matriarchal system (for example, the masculinisation of language in the use of pronouns such as "man" and "mankind"). Amadiume insists that such a system would be complimentary to patriarchy. Amadiume (1997, p. 101) postulates that:

> Patriarchy and matriarchy are social and political ideologies which directly decide the role and status of women in society, how society is to be organised and how social subjects are to relate to one another. They are also ideologies which decide the degree of violence and abuse of human rights that is permissible in society. Matriarchy, as was constructed by African women, had a very clear message about social and economic justice.

It must also be stated that feminism has not remained static in Africa and elsewhere. Rather, the feminist debate has continued to undergo a constant, definite metamorphosis in terms of: time (first, second, and third feminism waves), race (white women versus Black women), class (elite versus working-class women), culture (Western versus African), sexuality (straight women versus lesbian or transgender people), and religion (Christianity versus Islam) (Denzin and Lincoln, 2005; Gambaudo, 2007). The first two waves of feminism were mostly about attaining equal rights for women in civic and social terms. The claim to equality was viewed to mean that there is sameness between men and women. Women were expected to have male-like characteristics, such being as proactive, rational, and responsible, but still possessing their feminine side of being caring, maternal, and supportive. Second wave feminists rejected being defined as men, but rather as people with different needs. Effectively, they theorised the woman's situation. This gave birth to various forms of feminisms. Table 3.1, though not exhaustive, gives a breakdown of some of the dominant feminisms (Tisdell, 2008).

In all these phases and types, there are counter-arguments and conflicting positions but what is common among them is they all seem invested in challenging the oppression of women (Tisdell, 2008). The question of which women's stories or lived experiences are being told becomes critical, making this book contextually relevant and topical. It becomes an issue of representation, of who speaks on behalf of whom (Ang, 1996). The social media "talk" referred to in this book and the multiple forms of feminism that are used as interpretive lenses will help us to learn that women's experiences of GBV are different. There are now several other feminisms that have emerged throughout the world which are situated along geographical lines, such as Afro-feminism, South African feminism (Morrell, 2016), French Feminism (Gambaudo, 2007), and Australian feminism (Caine and Pringle, 1995), or along racial lines, such as Black feminism and Western feminism.

In the same vein, there is no single South African feminism, but many pluralistic and racially divided feminisms. Some scholars have used South Africa's localised circumstances and perspectives to come up with a "Southern theory" which is itself a version of South African feminism (Morrell, 2016,

Table 3.1 Dominant feminisms

Type of feminism	Description
Liberal	Generally, believes in equality. For instance, equal work for equal pay, but without taking a radical stance.
Radical	Sees patriarchy as the structural oppressor of women. Takes a radical stance.
Marxist	Sees power relations between dominant class groups as oppressors of women, on behalf of capitalism.
Socialist	Argues that it is not only patriarchy and capitalism that oppress women, but class and race.
Standpoint	Focuses on the role of power relations in shaping political knowledge.
Postmodern	Believes in the significance of hyperreal and free-floating signifiers of the individual, social structures, race, gender, class, and/or the forces of colonialism. These are intensified by digital technology.
Cyberfeminism	Concerned with how women occupy the technology space, and issues such as access and voice.
Black feminism	Rejects being defined from a Western perspective, but from its own Black or African identity.

p. 205). The book does not use the South African feminism theory because, again, one cannot pigeonhole all women since even though they may live in southern Africa, others in the same location may hold different views, hence the book includes different strands of feminisms. An expanded matrix of feminism allows us to see new things. For example, use of African feminism has in the past helped us to see how resistance against Apartheid in South Africa or the liberation struggle in Zimbabwe not only gave women a strong voice (Geisler, 2004), but essentially demonstrated how the tradition of female and gendered resistance to Western domination could be fruitfully traced to such heroines as Mbuya Nehanda, Modjadji, and Queen Nzinga, among others.

The so-called "Ubuntu feminism" (Connell and Van Marie, 2015) is another feminism with South African origins. It is grounded in the discourse of Ubuntu (*umuntu ngumuntu ngabantu* – "I am because we are") and is less panicked by the presence of patriarchy, but tries to negotiate within African traditional mores and realities. Ubuntu feminism is also not confined to the strictures of liberal feminism as drawn from second wave feminism. Rather, it offers (or the authors claim that it offers) an "authentic," or at least grounded, Southern African experiential lens that is more relevant to local conditions and histories. At least, such a theory promises to offer a local solution to the dilemmas that European and Western feminism cannot resolve. Nevertheless, just because Africa has homegrown feminist theories does not mean that they are acceptable to all.

The many feminisms are confirmation that Black feminism is by no means homogenous. Asserting the "blendedness" of Black feminism does not mean to say that Black women's experiences of oppression are monolithic. No feminist theory or brand of feminism is one size fits all, and none is justified in claiming what can only be a fake universality. Certainly, the diasporic Black feminists have a lot to learn from their African sisters. Amadiume has consistently argued that African feminism is not constrained by patriarchy, but rather, has its own strong countervailing matriarchy-based values that balance and counterbalance male–female power relations. Gender is not so much a war of the sexes (the classical Western Mars versus Venus binary) as a *negotiation*. Adesina and Adesina (2010, p. 2) point out that *matricentricity* in Amadiume's works accounts for the structural and ideological conditions of many African societies. Amadiume (1997) draws on the concepts of "matricentric unit" (1997, p. 18) or "matriarchal principle" (1997, p. 36) as her organising concepts to make sense of gender relations in Africa. African societies, she argues, are *structurally matricentric*, and our feminist analyses must start here. Oyewumi (2005), for her part, has argued that the category of "women" is not a synonym of gender in the African setting. That is, she argues that gender is not biologically determined, and social categories are not gender-specific. The categories "wife" and "husband," for instance, are not sex-specific (Oyewumi, 2005). Amadiume (1997) concurs. In Yoruba cosmology, for example, one cannot place a person in a certain category by merely looking at them. Rather, identity is more complex, context-specific, and grounded (Oyewumi, 2005). Oyewumi (2005) and Amadiume (1997) argue that African contexts can demonstrate the standard-ness of the assertion (first brought into the mainstream by Simone de Beauvoir) that gender is socially constructed, but that this critique is complicated by the fact that "gender was not an organizing principle in Yoruba society prior to colonization by the West. Rather, the primary principle of social organization was seniority defined by relative age" (Oyewumi, 1997, p. 31). If it is standard that gender is socially constructed, then gender cannot behave the same way across space, time, and culture.

When all is said and done, feminism has – as it were – come of age. Certainly, the span of feminist issues is now broader across a range of political, social, and cultural issues. There is space within feminism for a body of theory and politics that allows both for pluralism and difference (Brooks, 1997; Braithwaite, 2004). The politics of difference, as defined by Ang (1996), does not mean "giving up on community or solidarity sisterhood." For example, GBV is context-specific because women experience it differently which is what make it difficult to identify, particularly when it is subtle. Rather, the book agrees with Mekgwe (2008, p. 21) that there is a "need to espouse a theoretical model that is able to contain the varied positions; a model that will be fluid without being so pluralistic as to defy definition." As Spelman (1988, p. 14) contends, "even if we say all women are oppressed by sexism, we cannot automatically conclude that the sexism all women experience is the same."

At the same time, there is constant re-writing of feminism itself, because it is never static or fixed. Thus the "blended" choice in this book is made simply to find a theoretical starting point and theoretical coherence, without which the field of feminism becomes a conceptual jungle. It also serves to strengthen the book by accommodating as much of the Black female experience as possible. This view concurs with hooks (2000, p. 2), who points out that "without an agreed upon definition, we lack a sound foundation on which to construct theory or engage in overall meaningful praxis." It is in this sense that the UN's attempt to come up with a standard definition of violence against women has been regarded as a useful starting point (Geisler, 2004). The issues of feminism, representation, and online identity help to interpret the nature of contestations and struggles for meaning that occur on social media, and in the context of Black women, their voices have been mostly absent in media and public spaces. Black feminism is what the next section helps to define.

Black feminism

As stated in Chapter 1, very often when GBV is reported in South Africa, it is about influential women or based on how gruesome a murder is. It is seldom about marginalised Black women. It is this context and background that make Black feminism the most appropriate model for this book. Had this book not used this theoretical framework, the GBV that Gloria faces would remain invisible. Who speaks on social media, where power, ideology, and political economy are interrelated, is pivotal considering that GBV is often blamed on patriarchal power, as briefly discussed in Chapter 1. How women position themselves and "talk" about GBV on social media is therefore strategic and key. Since social media is relatively new, and it is books such as this one that examine patterns of "talk" on social media from a feminist point of view that will help to shed light on the nature of ideas emanating from such social platforms.

Black feminist theory is new, as it emerged from the 1980s and 1990s separately from the second wave feminism of the 1970s, which marginalised Black women. Black feminism on social media manifests itself through digital media activism like the #BlackLivesMatter and #MeToo campaigns. Another case in point, which will be discussed in the next chapter, is South Africa's #AmINext campaign against the murder of women. The ideas arising from localised campaigns such as #AmINext or *Scandal!*'s 16 Days of Activism episodes cited in this book are hardly documented or analysed. This book will thus help us to interpret meanings from such social media discourses. This is important because there has always existed a distorted picture of Black women in mainstream academia which has contributed to sidelining the Black female experience. In South Africa, a 2015 Global Media Monitoring Research study found that GBV stories made up a mere 1 per cent of the total stories covered in the mainstream media, yet a woman is murdered every three hours.

Black feminism is mostly associated with the interventions of Angela Davis, Patricia Hill Collins, bell hooks (hooks, as part of her identity politics, prefers that her name be spelt in lower-case letters), and Kimberlé Crenshaw, who coined the term *intersectionality* to refer to the multiform ways in which class, race, and gender are inextricably bound together. Angela Davis is famous as a former (incarcerated) Black Panther who has for her whole life fought against the structures of domination of Black people in America from the Civil Rights era to the contemporary era, where she writes and fights against the prison-industrial complex. Patricia Hill Collins came to prominent attention with her trailblazing text *Black Feminist Thought* (1990). Hill Collins's view of feminism, says Mekgwe (2008), is that "it is predominantly a white westernized experience that too often side-lines issues of racial difference, hence the imperative in her work to develop a Black feminist perspective which would more accurately reflect the realities and culture of Black women."

Black feminism is therefore a rejection of white feminism by women of colour in the United States drawing largely on the slave experience, but also on the Civil Rights era with the emergence of such figures as Rosa Parks. At the same time, the Civil Rights movement itself is seen as having marginalised women, thus Black feminism adds the Black female voice and experience to the Civil Rights discourse. Black men and women, though both are affected by racism, are affected in *gender-specific* ways. That is, racism has gender-specific contours. In Hill Collins's (2004, p. 5) view, these contours are more pronounced today, particularly at a time when racism is no longer as monolithic as in the 1960s.

Recognising that racism even exists remains a challenge for most white Americans, and increasingly for many African Americans as well. They believe that the passage of Civil Rights legislation eliminated racially discriminatory practices and that any problems Black people may experience now are of their own doing. Violations against Black men and women continue to occur, but one-third of African Americans have moved into the middle class, and Black people are more visible in positions of authority in schools, companies, hospitals, and government. Many Black people have difficulty seeing their connections to other Black people.

This is also the case in South Africa, where the end of Apartheid has brought about a generalised perception that racism is no longer as widespread as in the period before 1994. At the same time, privileged South Africans who live in the suburbs have seen their worlds morph into white worlds, and do not attach the same significance to racially discriminatory practices. Perceptions in the new South Africa have been changing. For example, whereas marriage is a dominant social practice among many older feminists, this view is not shared today by some women who now see it as "sleeping with the enemy" due to escalating femicide cases in the country. Interestingly, Hill Collins's comments were made in 2004. In the period 2015–2019, racism seems to have returned vigorously and become monolithic again, as signified by #BlackLivesMatter. Even in South Africa, incidents of racism trend in the news and social media with regularity. The contemporary #BlackLivesMatter movement can be traced to Black feminism as it has existed since the antebellum period in America.

Central to the articulation of Black feminism is the notion of Black female solidarity and Black sisterhood, which has been heightened by social media. As we will see in Chapters 4 and 5, platforms such as the *Scandal!* Facebook presence and #AmINext hashtag are more like help and counselling centres and spaces for women to share real-life examples with others in similar situations and people who can identify with the same pain. Solidarity is paramount because power over women and oppression of women have certainly proven to have multiple vectors (Crenshaw, 1989). The idea of Black *sisterhood* is important in healing fractures and division. Divide-and-rule tactics, after all, exacerbate the abuse of African/Black women as Morgan (1970) points out in her book of the same name, "sisterhood is powerful." The challenge of conceptualising feminism in Africa has been remarked upon (Nkealah, 2006), partly reflecting an anxiety to address the so-called crisis of "intellectual dependence" (Alatas, 2000). No one wants to be labelled unoriginal. "Feminist practitioners," as Mekgwe (2008, p. 12) points out, "did not simply seek to emulate their western feminist counterparts." As such, African feminists have sought to excavate local "libraries" (Zeleza, 2006b) that resonate with African realities, such as Tsitsi Dangarembga, Chimamanda Ngozi Adichie, Ifi Amadiume, and Oyeronke Oyewumi, to mention a few.

Since Western feminist research tended to identify all African women as one homogenous group (Antrobus, 2004, p. 124), African feminists have emphasised the "fluid character of African feminism" (Mekgwe, 2008, p. 11). The likes of Chioma Steady (1981), Amadiume (1997), and Oyewumi (2005), in this regard, have contributed to Black feminist theory in what I would call *an African key*. Their contributions specifically attempt to address and capture – in a nuanced way – the realities and cultures specific to Black women in Africa, particularly through the concepts of *matrifocality* or *matricentricity* (Adesina and Adesina, 2010), while at the same time producing an *epistemic rupture* from Western theories of gender. There is a danger that without the grounded interventions of African feminists, Black feminism will continue to be dominated by the diasporic strain, which is why this book is important because it adds to Indigenous feminist knowledges in sub-Saharan Africa about the intersection of GBV and social media which still has many unknowns. After all, Black women in Africa are often portrayed (or neglected) in Western feminism as a "powerless" group (Antrobus, 2004, p. 124). "Although agreeing with the politics of feminism," says Mekgwe (2008, p. 17), "most women writers in Africa have rejected the feminist while others have vacillated between endorsing the label and refuting it."

Fundamentally, I believe that the diversity in Black feminism – which makes us speak not just of Black feminism, but rather Black feminisms – is to be celebrated, rather than deplored. It is a strength rather than a weakness. Even men are now open to partnering with feminists, or even to calling themselves feminists and identifying publicly with the feminist agenda (Antrobus, 2004, pp. 148–149; Mekgwe, 2008, p. 17).

The ideas that emerge from the *Scandal!* Facebook page or #AmINext hashtag are certainly coming from both men and women, even though it is difficult to know the gender of people on social media. Speaking about GBV on social media is particularly sensitive and often stokes angry emotions, resulting in misogyny. But the generational clashes and misogynistic attacks are evidence that both men and women take part in the GBV "talk." In Chapter 5, we will see that although there is a clash of ideas, social media audiences generally have zero tolerance for GBV and have an awareness of GBV which suggests that men as much as women do not condone it. Black feminists such as hooks (1984) have long warned that an anti-men stance is broadly unproductive. In that regard, African feminism is viewed broadly as family-oriented, and whatever solutions that may be sought there cannot be complete without including the views of both men and women (cf. Mekgwe, 2008, p. 16). The exclusion of men will only serve to make things worse rather than better. Feminism in its orthodox and radical strain came to be framed as male-hating instead of just patriarchy-hating. Furthermore, not everyone is comfortable with the universal label "feminism." Rather, some people are more comfortable addressing issues to do with feminism without labelling them as such. As hooks in Antrobus (2004, p. 144) contends, "we can live and act in feminist resistance without ever using the word feminism." Antrobus argues that many distance themselves from it and yet use feminist analysis and strategies in their work. Ultimately, there is not much use fighting over labels if we are already persuaded that feminism materialises as *praxis*. Mekgwe (2008) emphasises that African feminism is not antagonistic to men, but rather challenges them to be aware of their complicity in women's subjugation so that they can better assist in dismantling gender-oppressive structures. A feminism that is anti-men would be rejected as un-African by the likes of Amadiume (1997) and Oyewumi (2005).

Nevertheless, African women's resistance to Western hegemony has shaped African feminism. This book locates African feminism as part of the same matrix of Black feminism. Whereas Black feminism has a strong and unmistakable diasporic (some would say Anglo-American) orientation, it is unnecessary to divide the struggles of Black women based on geography. Black women's oppression is shifting all the time and becoming more complex, and it is not necessary for Black women to fight over boundaries, especially regarding an issue such as GBV which is a global menace. If anything, this book teaches us that regardless of the beliefs women hold, there is no opposition among women to the idea that GBV is an oppression that violates women's rights. What differ are the definitions and methods used to combat it.

The choice of the blended Black feminist theory in this book necessarily centres Africa and the experiences of African women, for obvious reasons. Oyewumi (2005, p. 9), for instance, stresses that the study of gender in Africa, if it is to be relevant, needs to be based on the ideas that originate from the continent, which is what this book is about. Chioma Steady (1981) regards African feminism as emphasising female autonomy and co-operation, nature over culture, the centrality of children, multiple mothering, and kinship (Mekgwe, 2008, p. 16). Renowned Afrocentrist Cheikh Anta Diop (1989) has emphasised the need for African people to be understood "within their own self-constructed status and identity and as creators of their nations," thus there was a political choice to use the term Black feminism interchangeably with African feminism in this book.

A Black feminist lens is critical if we consider the perspective of those who argue that African identities have been eroded due to the destruction of family institutions through capitalism and colonialism which also rendered women as minors, resulting in their becoming invisible and voiceless. Some also feel that in Africa, masculinity is not the biggest threat to women, but rather colonialism. Ntuli (2018) argues that we have become obsessed over and fear African masculinities as if this is the root of the problem. Ntuli (2018) says that it is the colonial patriarchal mentality that has reproduced the conservative male gaze across centuries and has stripped African women of their dignity and voice. It is this mentality that positions men like Obakeng as superior to women like Gloria. Unlike the radical feminists, African feminists are comfortable with the idea that men *are part of the solution*. It may be the case that, as Antrobus (2004) suggests, men who are willing to identify publicly with the feminist agenda are very rare, but ultimately feminism as a political project must be broad-based as opposed to elitist. Digital media activism is helping to bring out many voices, including those that were not heard before.

Mann (2014) examined the question, "What can feminism learn from new media?" He observed that traditional mass media and academia have "historically excluded, silenced, or heavily mediated/edited the words of Black women." It is therefore vital to examine the content of these media platforms and channels (Mann, 2014). The term "new media" may imply there are a lot of new things that we still need to learn from, particularly from a feminist perspective.

Although many women are no longer restricted to the home (or the kitchen), they still face exploitation through pervasive patriarchal social and economic structures. These include new technologies such as online and digital technology. Analysing this book from just a Black feminist angle without considering how women talk on social media would not give us a complete picture of the feminist digital media activism articulated by this book. Cyberfeminism is a critical topic because digital media activism depends on it.

Cyberfeminism

The internet is a defining medium of our modern times because it is a medium of both mass and personal communication (McQuail, 2010, p. 41). Participating on the internet has given rise to cyberculture. Cyberculture defines the various social and cultural phenomena that arise from the widespread use of information technology in modern society (Negroponte, 1995; Castells, 1996, 2001). Chatting on social media, for instance, is an instance of cyberculture. The interest in this book goes further than just an interest in the cyberculture of social media "talk," to explore the dynamics of such interaction in relation to intimate partner violence. The term "cyberculture" is a portmanteau of "cyberspace" and "culture." Hawthorne and Renate explain that "cyberspace" refers to widespread, interconnected digital technology.[2] They point out that the term "cyber" is a Greek word for "governor" or "gubernatorial." Hawthorne and Renate further elaborate that the original meaning of "cyber" is to "steer," as one would "steer a boat." Its connection to technology is in "navigation, mapping, steering one's way through the World Wide Web." The vital aspect is who governs it (Hawthorn and Renate, 1999). There is a myth that the internet is self-governing, but is it? This is a pertinent question in relation to GBV social discourse in southern Africa.

Wolmark (2003) has characterised cyberspace as a "tool to examine our very sense of reality," a point that has seen feminists taking up space to raise subject that are hard to deal with, such as GBV. The relationship between feminist theory and cyberculture is complex for the reason mentioned earlier, that the oppression of women persists through pervasive patriarchal social and economic structures. Chapter 2 outlined the concern that GBV "talk" among marginalised women as discussed in this book goes on without the participation of the targeted women due to lack of access to the internet, smartphones, and data. There is a tendency to think that technology is neutral, value-free, and innocent. It is not. Rather, it is implicated with power and power relations, which is why, on one hand, digital technology is a tool for women's empowerment, access, and participation (Hawthorne and Renate, 1999, p. 2), but on the other, it is also an instrument for oppression. The misogyny that is experienced both on the *Scandal!* Facebook page and the #AmINext hashtag shows that digital technologies are weapons for gender violence and exploitation (Stormer, 2004). Yet many people now turn first and increasingly to the internet when searching for information or expressing themselves (Hinman, 2005). Digital media activism thrives on the internet, but there are also concerns that the digital divide behind the inequality in accessing information on the internet may affect women acutely since they are traditionally excluded from being at the centre of productive relations (Segev, 2010). In fact, this was one of the limitations of the data analysed for this book, as the chances are that cases of GBV and social media conversations on the topic leave out the participation of Black marginalised women. Women may either have their opinions ignored or shouted down in important online conversations, or they may be unable to access the internet altogether.

Cyberfeminism is a variant of feminism which acknowledges the differences in power between men and women in technologically dominated digital discourse (Hawthorne and Renate, 1999, p. 2). Early studies on cyberfeminism centred on the masculinisation of cyberspace, citing women's access to technology as a huge limiting factor in terms of women creating their own definitions (Segev, 2010). Cyberfeminists consider the internet to be a masculine space within which access and the agency of women are limited, but this may not necessarily be the case now. Past studies of the masculinisation of the cyberspace, for instance, acknowledge that knowledge is socially constructed, and gender is crucial to that construction (Wolmark, 2003). Maynard (1998) notes that the gendered nature of scientific knowledge seeks to take account of the way in which knowledge both produces and is produced by existing relations of power. Some early studies suggested that women were reluctant to go online, were less confident of their abilities when they did so, were less participatory in online discussion groups, and were less represented among computer network policy makers and designers than men (Herring, 1996). Some of these early studies even went to the extent of citing the fear of having their devices infected by computer viruses as one way in which cybertechnology can scare women away from participating fully in digital spaces, thus perpetuating masculine control. With the near inevitability of internet use across the world, the fear of the internet by women suggested by these early studies seems dated.

Cyberfeminist research in general starts from a point of view of assessing how and why women use computer technologies. For instance, Guntarik and Trott (2016) examined what forms of online political participation existed among Thai women. As cyberfeminism is concerned with the voice or voicelessness of women online, it utilises approaches that regard the internet as a public sphere, counter-public sphere, or feminine (or female-friendly) space (Gajjala, 2004). The issue of online spaces as a public sphere for women considers the issue of women-centred online spaces where women may contribute their views in safe environments. Gajjala has argued that:

> When we speak of women centred environment there is an implicit assumption that there will be wonderful conflict-free spaces. Yet are not the unsaid conditions for the erasure of conflict and the creation of consensus equal to the erasure of dissenting voices and the performances of a lack of hierarchy based on the silence of many others?
>
> (2004, p. 76)

Gajjala (2004), who researched specific online debates about women's issues, wanted to find out how much internet access women had and whether they were finding a "space from which to speak." What kinds of discourses are marginalised? What complicities and resistances get articulated through the struggles for control over meaning in such spaces? Who is absented, disappeared, silenced, and why? As we will see in the next chapters, both the Facebook and Twitter platforms discussed in this book serve as educational forums and public spheres, but also as tools for women's oppression. Thus, the internet has been seen as a space that is empowering of diverse discourses and marginalised groups (Creswell, 2009), but also as one that can harm "talk." This is because patriarchy and masculinity may also be reproduced online. Hall (1996) observed that:

> Male participants are said to accomplish this by ignoring the topics which women introduce, producing conversational floors based on hierarchy instead of collaboration, dismissing women's responses as irrelevant, and contributing a much higher percentage of the total number of postings and text produced.
>
> (Hall, 1996, p. 154)

The aspect of discourse in cyberculture is particularly important because people appear to have different communication strategies online and offline. As the interface between the body and technology is redefined, cyberfeminism has also become interested in the internet as a bodiless space where gender swapping is possible. This interest is associated with the cybertheories of Donna Haraway (1991), for whom cyberfeminism is anchored in postmodern feminist thought. Cybertheory has brought to the fore the issue of the collapse of boundaries and fixed categories of meaning due to the proliferation of online worlds. For instance, when texting or chatting online, the body is apparently freed from the physical and completely enters the realm of the *symbolic*, or the symbolic real (Reid, 1994). In this symbolic realm, textual bodies move freely and imaginatively "with a fluidity that does not seem to have any limits" (Reid, 1994). It seems as if the physical body ceases to exist. There is thus an aspect of freedom associated with being online. There is, however, some dispute about whether physical bodies get erased when we are online (Hall, 1996). This last aspect about "bodiless consciousnesses" leads us to the final element of my blended feminist approach that is utilised in this book: postmodern (and deconstructionist) feminism, which is discussed next.

Postmodern feminism

Postmodern feminism is not easy to define (Gens, 2009) and does not offer neat answers. What it is considered by its proponents to be good at is putting a range of complex and thought-provoking questions out there. It does not seem to me to be a new feminism, but rather one that holds potential for ceaseless innovation. Hence:

> Postmodern feminism's changeable life indicates a move away from easy categorisations and binaries, including the dualistic patterns of (male) power and (female) oppression on which much feminist thought, and politics are built.
>
> (Gens, 2009, p. 24)

The polysemy offered by postmodernity allows for a "recognition of the presence of power in the formation of knowledge and an understanding that the self is socially constructed in the context of narratives created by society and the self" (East, 1998). "Talk" about GBV is not just any discussion about a social problem, but is a rejection of patriarchy and the status quo. It is a challenge to all systems of power that give rise to GBV, including governance. *Scandal!* episodes of violence are a feminist political statement demanding change in how GBV is treated in the South Africa. As we saw in Chapter 1, some cases of violence against women go unreported because of lack of faith in the justice system. Welded into this approach is a deconstruction perspective which seeks to expose "supposed truths and grand systems of belief by unravelling a text to reveal its assumptions, contradictions, or inconsistencies" (East, 1998). The purpose of deconstruction, as East says, is "to create multiple meanings and to determine perspectives that are marginalized or not named." Postmodern feminism offers a renewed meaning which shows that there is no one single hegemonic truth but, rather, multiple realities (Kostikova, 2013; East, 1998). For example, digital media activists on the *Scandal!* page and #AmINext hashtag present varied views on GBV-related topics such as marriage, inheritance, and the woman's place in marriage while at the same time agreeing that GBV is wrong. A postmodern-inflected critique also considers how new media and cyberculture give individuals autonomy to express their views on GBV in ways that never existed before social media. For example, it was rare for women to speak out about their marital problems in public because there were no places like social media that enabled conversation to take place without being constrained by geography or time.

Critics note, of course, the danger of distortions within the "post"-feminisms that may be read as alternatives (or even contrary) to feminism and its social and political agenda. They are also wary of the circulation of a kind of "free market feminism" that "sells women an illusion of progress by appropriating and co-opting feminist notions of empowerment and choice" (Genz, 2009, p. 21). However, "post"-feminism does not parade itself as an alternative to feminism, but rather advances an alternative understanding and aids a new construction of feminine identity (Kostikova, 2013). It gives people freedom of choice. For example, Gloria is considered a renegade because she does not conform to patterns of how society expects a married woman to behave. That is, "post"-feminism should not be taken to mean feminism ceases to be a political movement aimed at social justice.

Rather, it emphasises situatedness, within a specific time and place (Genz, 2009). It is this time and place that has been fragmented by the logics of Facebook ("Likes," "friending," "unfriending," and so on). How does the time and "place" (or placelessness) of Facebook change the way we "talk"? Is "talk" on Facebook placeless?

To some, such as Denfeld (1995, p. 2), the term postmodern feminism suggests an "ending" to feminism or its "failure" and loss of validity. Such an end comes about because there has allegedly been an overachievement of feminism, to the extent that feminism is no longer relevant in young women's lives because there are equal opportunities everywhere. However, this is not necessarily true. The quest for gender equality and to end gender violence is even more urgent today (Geisler, 2004). We saw in Chapter 1 that in South Africa, GBV is "hyperendemic." The #AmINext campaign suggests fear and urgency in the GBV situation in South Africa. As noted earlier, research shows that women remain easy targets of violence, exclusion, victimisation, and abuse. Furthermore, gendered violence is often systemic. As Walby (1990, p. 201) points out, women's household production, paid work, the state, male violence, sexuality, and culture all together "capture the depth, pervasiveness and interconnectedness of women's subordination." This explains why GBV remains complex to solve. Some battles might have been won, but one senses that it is disingenuous to declare the war is won. While there may be a general acknowledgement of feminist rights in many African countries, women are still generally discriminated against and the provision of equal opportunities across the socio-political and economic strata is still limited to interventions such as women's quotas.

Many African countries have enacted laws against domestic violence, but have not provided environments and spaces that allow many women to take advantage of these laws. Part of the problem seems to be a lack of knowledge about these laws and interventions, as well as fear of reporting cases, and male chauvinistic attitudes at police stations and courts (Sibanda-Moyo et al., 2017). South Africa, as noted, has one of the highest incidences of domestic violence in the world – evidence of persistence of violence against women which affects women's participation in all sectors of society. An area seemingly as mundane as the sharing of views and opinions bespeaks the nature of the silences that women find themselves relegated to. Institutions such as the Graça Machel Trust, a Pan African civic society non-governmental organisation on women's and children's issues with a presence in 16 African countries, has formed women's networks in various sectors of the economy to leverage opportunities for women.[3] Such initiatives point to the dearth of opportunities for women and the states of repression of women's rights in many African countries. In fact, Antrobus (2004) and Geisler (2004) draw our attention to a reality of underachievement in women's movements. At least, they argue that young women in Africa no longer see women's movements as relevant, or they feel excluded, but the advent of digital media feminist activism is changing this perception. Hashtags, for example, are a means of spreading feminist ideas and resolving issues that are common such as GBV. The book has already alluded to digital media campaigns such as #MeToo and #BlackLivesMatter. But Braithwaite's (2004) assertion that feminism may leave women in an ambivalent space where they feel it guarantees their being included yet they still experience a reality of being excluded is still true. There is also the ambivalence of being acknowledged and paid tribute to and accepted, and yet at the same time refuted and rebuffed. As we will see in the next chapter, laws to deal with domestic violence may be put in place, but institutionalised patriarchy remains an obstacle to controlling GBV.

Feminism is thus not dead, but it needs to do more to find increased relevance, and digital media activism is a means to achieve that. Feminism's status as a frame of reference, an explanatory principle, and the basis of activism is currently not assured. It is important for Black women to develop, as Abrahams (2001) says, a sense of full individuality in a world where their experience of *self* has been over-determined by external definitions of their identity which are racist and sexist. Individual women still need to have their personal choices respected, and to have the recognition of their rights and independence respected in general society (Denfeld, 1995, p. 2). This development of a self and of individuality is the one that the character of Gloria, in the *Scandal!* episodes under discussion, struggles to attain due to Obakeng's sexist violence. But are we going anywhere with digital activism? The next chapter will help us to answer that question.

Notes

1 http://whomakesthenews.org/gmmp/gmmp-reports/gmmp-2015-reports.
2 Hawthorne, S., & Renate, K, (2013) *Cyberfeminism*, https://ces260jh.files.wordpress.com/2013/01/hawthorne-klein.pdf/. Accessed 12 January 2019.
3 One of these networks is the Women in Media Network that was specifically created to change the narrative of women in traditional and new media, including social media (*Graça Machel Trust 2015 Annual Report*). The idea is that conversations women may carry on these media platforms will help shape and define the sort of identities that women in Africa want to be associated with.

References

Abrahams, Y. (2001). Learning by doing: Notes towards the practice of womanist principles in the 'new' South Africa. *Agenda*, 50. https://doi.org/10.1080/10130950.2001.9675995.

Adesina, O. (2010). Re-appropriating Matrifocality: Endogeneity and African gender scholarship. *African Sociological Review*, 14(1), 2–19.

Alatas, S.F. (2000). Academic dependency in the social sciences. *American Studies International*, 38(2), 80–96.

Amadiume, I. (1997). *Reinventing Africa: Matriarchy, religion & culture*. London: Zed Books.
Ang, I. (1996). *Living room wars: Rethinking media audiences for a post-modern world*. London: Routledge.
Antrobus, P. (2004). *The global women's movement: Origins, issues and strategies*. New York: St Martins Press.
Baudrillard, J. (1991). *The gulf war did not take place*. Translated by P. Patton. Indianapolis, IN: Indiana University Press.
Baym, N.K. (2000). *Tune in, Log on: Soaps, fandom and online community*. London: Sage Publications.
Blumenthal, D. (1997). *Women and soap opera: A cultural feminist perspective*. London: Praeger Publishers.
Braithwaite, A. (2004). Politics of/and backlash. *Journal of International Women's Studies*, 5(5), 18–33.
Britton, H. (2006). Organising against gender violence in South Africa. *Journal of Southern African Studies*, 32(1), 145–163.
Brooks, A. (1997). *Postfeminisms: Feminism, cultural theory, and cultural forms*. London: Routledge.
Caine, B., & Pringle, R. (Eds). (1995). *Transitions: New Australian feminisms*. Sydney: Allen & Unwin.
Castells, M. (1996). *The rise of the network society: The information age: Economy, society, and culture*, Volume 1. Oxford: Blackwell Publishers.
Castells, M. (2001). *The internet galaxy: Reflections on the internet, business and society*. Oxford: Oxford University Press.
Choja, O., & Nelson, O. (2016). Psychological violence and the bane of cyber-harassment against women: An experiential inquest on Facebook. *Gender & Behaviour*, 14(3), 7589–7608. Academic Search Complete, EBSCOhost, viewed 18 July 2017.
Crenshaw, K.W. (1989). Demarginalizing the intersection of race and sex: A black feminist critique of antidiscrimination doctrine, Feminist theory, and antiracist politics. *University of Chicago Legal Forum*, 1989, 139–167.
Creswell, J.W. 2009. *Research design: Qualitative, quantitative, and mixed methods approaches* (Third Edition). Thousand Oaks, CA: Sage.
Cornell, D., & van Marle, K. (2015). Ubuntu feminism: Tentative reflections. *Verbum Et Ecclesia*, 36(2), 1–8, Academic Search Complete, EBSCOhost, viewed 17 June 2017.
Davis, A., & Tadia, N. (2005). *Beyond the frame: Women of color and visual representation*. New York: Palgrave Macmillan.
DeFrancisco, V. (1997). Gender, power and practice: Or, putting your money (and your research) where your mouth is. In Wodak, R. (Ed), *Gender and discourse*. London: Sage Publications Ltd, pp. 37–56, viewed 30 May 2018, https://doi.org/10.4135/9781446250204.n3.
Denfeld, R. (1995). *The new Victorians: A young woman's challenge to the new feminist order*. New York: Warner Books.
Denzin, N.K., & Lincoln, Y.S. (2005). Introduction. In Denzin, N.K., & Lincoln, Y.S. (Eds). *The Sage handbook of qualitative research* (Third Edition). Thousand Oaks, CA: Sage, pp. 1–32.

Diop, C.A. (1989). *The cultural unity of Black Africa: The domains of matriarchy and of patriarchy in classical antiquity.* London: Karnak House.

East, J.F. (1998). In-dependence: A feminist postmodern deconstruction. *Affilia: Journal of Women & Social Work,* 13(3), 273–288. Academic Search Complete, EBSCOhost, viewed 14 July 2017.

Fourie, P.J. (2008). *Media studies: Policy, management, and media representation.* Cape Town: Juta.

Gajjala, A. (2004). *Cyber selves: Feminist ethnographies or South Asian women.* New York: Altamira space.

Gambaudo, S.A. (2007). French feminism vs Anglo-American feminism: A reconstruction. *European Journal of Women's Studies,* 14(2), 93–180.

Genz, S. (2009). *Post-femininities in popular culture.* London: Palgrave Macmillan.

Geisler, G. (2004). *Women and the remaking of politics in Southern Africa: Negotiating autonomy, incorporation, and representation.* Spain: Grafilur Artes Gráficas.

Giddens, A. (1989). *Sociology.* Oxford: Blackwell/Polity.

Guntarik, O., & Trott, V. (2016). Changing media ecologies in Thailand: Women's online participation in the 2013/2014 Bangkok protests. *Austrian Journal of South-East Asian Studies / Österreichische Zeitschrift Für Südostasienwissenschaften,* 9(2), 235–251. Academic Search Complete, EBSCOhost, viewed 18 July 2017.

Global Media Monitoring Project. (2015). *Who makes the news?* London: World Association for Christian Communication. Home page. https://www.media-diversity.org/additional-files/Who_Makes_the_News_-_Global_Media_Monitoring_Project.pdf. Accessed 2018/02/21.

Hall, K. (1996). Cyberfeminism. In Herring, S. (Ed), *Computer-mediated communication: Linguistic, social and Cross-cultural perspectives.* Amsterdam: John Benjamins, pp. 147–170.

Haraway, D. (1991). A cyborg manifesto: Science technology and socialist-feminism in the late twentieth century. In Hobson, D. (Eds), *Simians cyborgs and women: The reinvention of nature.* New York: Routledge, pp. 149–181.

Hawthorne, S., & Renate, K. (Eds). (1999). *Cyberfeminism, connectivity, critique and creativity.* Melbourne: Spinifex Press.

Herring, S. (1996). Posting in a different voice: Gender and ethics in computer mediated communication. In Ess, C. (Ed), *Philosophical approaches to computer mediated.* Amsterdam: John Benjamins, pp. 115–145.

Hill Collins, P. (1990). *Black feminist thought: Knowledge, consciousness, and the politics of empowerment.* Boston, MA: Unwin Hyman.

Hill Collins, P. (2004). *Black sexual politics: African Americans, gender, and the new racism.* London: Routledge.

Hinman, L.M. (2005). Esse est indicato in Google: Ethical and political issues in search engines. *International Review of Information Ethics* 3: 20–25.

hooks, b. (1982). *Ain't I a Woman: Black women and feminism.* Boston, MA: South End Press.

hooks, b. (2000). *Feminism is for everybody: Passionate politics.* London: Pluto Press.

hooks, b. (1984). *Feminist theory from margin to centre.* Boston, Masachusettes: South End Press.

Howarth, C. (2011). Representations, identity, and resistance in communication. In Hook, D., Franks, B., & Bauer, M. W. (Eds), *The social psychology of communication*. London: Palgrave Macmillan.

Kostikova, A. (2013). Postmodernism: A feminist critique. *Metaphilosophy*, 44(1/2), 24–28. Academic Search Complete, EBSCOhost, viewed 14 July 2017.

Mahlaba, G. (2023). WhatsApp interview. Johannesburg. 14 February. Interview notes available from the author.

Mann, K.L. (2014). What can feminism learn from new media? *Communication & Critical/Cultural Studies*, 11(3), 293–297, Communication & Mass Media Complete, EBSCOhost, viewed 17 June 2017.

Maynard, M. (1998). Women's studies. In Jackson, S., & Jones, J. (Eds), *Contemporary feminist theories*. Edinburgh: Edinburgh University Press.

McFadden, P. (2007). African feminist perspectives of post-coloniality: The black scholar. *The Struggle in Zimbabwe*, 37(1), 36–42. Accessed 2016/05/09.

McLaurin, I. (Ed). (2001). *Black feminist anthropology: Theory, politics, praxis, and poetics*. New Brunswick, NJ: Rutgers University Press.

McQuail, D. (2010). *McQuail's mass communication theory*. London: Sage.

Mekgwe, P. (2008). Theorising African feminism(s): The 'colonial' question. *An African Journal of Philosophy*, XX, 11–22.

Mikell, G. (1997). Conclusions: Theorising and strategizing about African women and state crisis. In Mikell, G. (Ed), *African feminism: The politics of survival in Sub-Saharan Africa*. Philadelphia: University of Pennsylvania Press, pp. 333–346.

Modleski, T. (1979). The search for tomorrow in today's soap operas: Notes on a feminine narrative form. *Film Quarterly*, 33(1), 12–21.

Mohanty, C.T., Russo, A., & Torres, L. (Eds). (1991). *Third world women and the politics of feminism*. Bloomington and Indianapolis, IN: Indiana University Press.

Morgan, R. (1970). *Sisterhood is powerful: An anthology of writings from the women's liberation movement*. New York: Random House.

Morrell, R. (2016). Making Southern theory? Gender researchers in South Africa. *Feminist Theory*, 17(2), 191–209. https://doi.org/10.1177/1464700116645877.

Nkealah, N. (2006). Conceptualizing feminism(s) in Africa: The challenges facing African women writers and critics. *English Academy Review: Southern African Journal of English Studies*, 23(1), 133–141.

Negroponte, N. (1995). *Being digital*. New York: Alfred A. Knopf.

Ntuli, P. (2018). Nonkanyiso Chonco: Othered to sustain our public gaze at Zuma. Home page. https://mg.co.za/article/2018-04-28-00-nonkanyiso-chonco-othered-to-sustain-our-public-gaze-at-zuma. Accessed 2018/05/24.

Oyewumi, O. (1997). *The invention of women: Making an African sense of western gender discourse*. Minneapolis, MN: University of Minnesota Press.

Oyewumi, O. (2005). Visualising the body: Western theories and African subjects. In Oyewumi, O. (Ed), *African gender studies: A reader*. Basingstoke, Great Britain: Palgrave Macmillan, pp. 3–21.

Pilcher, J., & Whelehan, I. (2004). *Fifty key concepts of gender studies*. London: Sage Publications.

Pillay, A. (2010). Women's activism and transformation: Arising from the cusp. *Feminist Africa*, 14, 63–78.

Reid, J. (1994). Responding to ESL students' texts: The myths of appropriation. *Tesol Quarterly*, 28(2), 273–292.

Segev, E. (2010). *Google and the digital divide: The bias of online knowledge*. Oxford: Chandos Publishing.

Sibanda-Moyo, N., Konje, E., & Brobbey, M.K. (2017). *Violence against women in South Africa: A country in crisis 2017*. Johannesburg: Centre for the Study of Violence and Reconstruction.

Spelman, E. (1988). *Inessential woman: Problems of exclusion in feminist thought*. Boston, MA: Beacon Press.

Steady, F.C. (Ed). (1981). *The Black women cross-culturally*. Cambridge: Schenkman Publishing Company.

Stone, A.R. (1995). *The war of desire and technology at the close of the mechanical age*. Cambridge, MA: The MIT Press.

Stormer, N. (2004). Articulation: A working paper on rhetoric and taxis'. *Quarterly Journal of Speech*, 90(3), 257–284.

Sunden, J. (2002). Textual talk and typed bodies in online interaction. *Talking Gender and Sexuality*, 94, 289.

Tisdell, E.J. (2008). Feminist epistemology. InGiven, L.M. (Ed), *The Sage encyclopaedia of qualitative research methods*, Volumes 1 & 2. London: Sage, pp. 331–333.

Turkle, S. (1995). *Life on the screen: Identity in the age of the Internet*. New York: Simon & Schuster Paperbacks.

Vasilescu, B., Capiluppi, A., & Serebrenik, A. (2012). Gender, representation, and online participation: A quantitative study of stack overflow, social informatics 2012 International Conference on social informatics. Proceedings of a conference, IEEE Computer Society, Washington, DC, pp. 332–338.

Walby, S. (1990). *Theorising patriarchy*. Oxford: Blackwell.

Wiese, M., Lauer, J., Pantazis, G., & Samuels, J. (2014). Social networking experiences on Facebook: A survey of gender differences amongst students'. *Acta Commercii* 14(1), Art. #218, 7 pages. https://actacommercii.co.za/index.php/acta/article/view/218/345.

Wolmark, J. (2003). The pleasure-pain of feminist politics in the 1970s. In Graham, H., Kaloski, A. N., & Robertson, E. (Eds), *"The Feminist Seventies."*. Illinois: University of Illinois Press.

Woodward, K. (2002). *Understanding identity*. London: Arnold.

Zeleza, P.T. (2006b). The disciplinary, interdisciplinary and global dimensions of African studies. *International Journal of African Renaissance Studies*, 1(2), 195–220.

4 Gender digital activism offline and online GBV "talk"

Introduction

An examination into the so-called "online" and "offline" and how they have merged and become virtually unrecognisable is relevant and key to this chapter. Partly, the issue of "online" and "offline" boils down to whether we can, and how far we can, step outside social media to see the world from a non-social media point of view, and vice versa. The notion of "talk" is predicated on the "old," which is a reference to traditional – or offline – modes of discourse, but has been so diffracted by the "new" of online platforms that it is scarcely recognisable as "talk."

If we want to believe that new forms of identity are possible on, and because of, social media, and indeed are being asserted and negotiated on social media, then perhaps social media "talk" cannot ground itself in anything other than social media. There is a binarity created here between the real world out there (let us call it the "outside") where violence takes place and where the real victims live, and the world that is available only if one is logged on (let us call it the "inside"), where commenters go and express themselves about GBV. The binarity of "inside" and "outside" may mean that we are called upon to respond uniquely to the ways in which social media functions as a signifying practice. I can go as far as to say that social media, as a *signifying practice*, can stand on its own *apart* from how we "talk" and socialise in the "real world" – both in a positive and negative way. Social media "talk" may not be a mere reflection of an already existing, lived, social reality (reality "out there"), but rather constitutes an authentic new layer of reality that is available (only) once someone is *logged on* and *signed in* to Facebook or Twitter.

We must not look too much for answers externally. Rather, the answers about how people "talk" and why they "talk" the way they do are there on social media. The "language" of Facebook, for instance, is a system of Facebook-based signs and signifiers, located on the "inside" of Facebook, each of which acquires its identity in relation to the identity of other Facebook-based signs and signifiers – such that social media "talk" comes into existence largely (perhaps exclusively?) through signification. We must learn, ontologically, to be on Facebook (to be on the "inside"), and internalise what it means to

DOI: 10.4324/9781003260820-4

be on Facebook, even if Facebook is not a "real" place. We must learn ways of being "inside" Facebook, even as we also exist out there in the real world (being on the "outside").

The discourse of "outside" and "inside" is inherently about the nature of meaning, which we know qualitative research is best at uncovering. By talking about "outside" and "inside," we are also initiating an examination into the ontology of Facebook. Is social media a real place? Is it a placeless place? Are there real people on social media? Is the subject on Facebook (the subject on the "inside") the same subject on the "outside" (in the real world out there)? Is the Facebook "friend" even a subject, or merely one of many dispersed subjectivities? How should we treat what an avatar says? Should we treat it as proper discourse? Such questions are complicated by algorithms and bots that are machines that can themselves organise and generate forms of "talk" that seem as good as, if not better than, those of "real" human beings. Ultimately, what we are interrogating here is the validity of studying Facebook comments, and whether it amounts to anything. At the one end, the issue is about qualitative methods and how much science they contain, and if we can reliably learn anything about society from them. At the other end is the theme of gender violence itself, and what (or whether) we can learn about it from simply scrolling up and down on a social media platform, and a better way to find out is in the study of the social media tools such as Twitter and Facebook.

We know, for instance, that being a "friend" on Facebook (on the "inside"), for instance, is not the same as being friends in the real world (on the "outside"). Being friends in the real world (on the "outside") requires a different type and different amount of commitment that is not possible on social media (on the "inside"). A hashtag is not action, perhaps because it is all on the "inside." We saw with the #BringBackOurGirls movement, for instance, that those who wanted the girls to be brought back would not have recognised any of the Chibok girls even if they had met them on the street (the typical criticism of clicktivism and "keyboard warriors"). One of the weaknesses of digital media activism is when it becomes just clicktivism that has no social impact. Just because we express our views on social media does not necessarily make things so. Some may argue that the universe has not really changed; only our hashtags have proliferated and trended. "Liking" something on Facebook is not the same as liking something in the real world, partly because liking something in the real world takes a lot more than just an emoticon or emoji. Just because someone says something negative or positive about Gloria or Obakeng on Facebook does not mean that the same person, in the real world, may be saying the same things or holding the same opinions. Ultimately, identities are grounded in social practice, not on hashtags or emojis. As Sayyid and Zac (1998, p. 255) point out, the labels we use to understand reality are not the labels of reality itself. Because of the inevitable distance that exists between "outside" and "inside," it seems that all we can uncover through social media "talk" is an interpretation of, as Sayyid and Zac (1998, p. 265) would put it, "the way a specific discourse is constructed: how identities are constituted, how narratives are articulated, and how the ensemble of narratives is rendered coherent." We can never proceed to an experience or even a knowledge of what gender violence is really like on the "outside" (in the real world out there), make empirical claims about gender violence, nor claim access to the authentic feelings and inner thoughts of those posting things on Facebook.

While we dismiss the possibility of finding any "outside" (the real world) in the "inside" (Facebook), it is important to recognise that people are inherently unique and different, thus the reasons they say what they say and how they say what they say can never be rendered completely transparent – even if these things are expressed on the self-same platform. Just because people say things on social media does not make interpretation suddenly effortless. Just because people say things on Facebook does not make such "talk" homogenous or monolithic. There is still room to discover the complexity of social media. Indeed, this is the rationale and justification behind this book. Even as we concede that identities are grounded in social practice, and not on hashtags or emojis, there is a lot more than meets the eye on social media – Facebook, Twitter, Instagram, WhatsApp, and so on – in terms of richness, complexity, and "thick descriptions" of human behaviours. Basically, treating social media "talk" as signifying practice means that whatever data we mine from social media is richer and far more complex than it would be if we treated social media as a mere mechanical medium containing strings of letters, words, and statements. Hence, social media "talk," even if grounded only on social media, does not permit us to impose uniformity on what people say, even if people are saying what they are saying on the very same platform (in this case, Facebook) and using the very same tools. "Social depth" might not be what Zuckerberg's soulless algorithms built into social media, but wherever people congregate and "talk," there is always signification.

It is thus the crucial element of signification that not only unites the "inside" and "outside," but brings social depth to what seem to be the chaotic threads of Facebook comments. Such social depth was never originally there, is not always there, is by no means automatic, and is not inevitably there. This is where the power of qualitative methods comes into its own, because they always leave room for human subjectivities and agency. What qualitative methods offer is a different – even *unique* – way of seeing, and reflecting about, the world. They address concerns from an entirely different perspective. I prefer the perspective that says that life is not like a game of chess. Rather, beyond schemas and formulas, things are complex and complicated. Human beings are not just statistics, schemas, numerical formulae, or lab specimens. Social media "talk" is still about humans talking, not some social media specimens. The idea of this book was to come away with, to recover and to fulfil, a distinct sense of politics from my study of social media.

As Kozinets (2010, p. 8; see also Kozinets, 2015, p. 92) says, netnography not only helps give the researcher a cultural understanding of human experiences, drawn from online social integration and content, but also an understanding of a "hidden world" that may not seem to be there at face value. The study which informs this book succeeded in making visible the links between representation (*Scandal!*), subjectivity (audience "talk" about *Scandal!*), and politics (my critique of the gender violence). The success of this book, whether or not it is framed as a political project, is not minimised by the fact that I scraped my "data" from Facebook or Twitter instead of interviewing "real" South African women who experience intimate partner violence. If anything, the book benefits from the uniqueness of such data.

The interpretive plane of signification has introduced a new dimension: it means that "outside" and "inside" are no longer separate. The sharp distinction and *a priori* separation between them has fallen away. Instead, in place of that split, one can start to "talk" about (i) *Scandal!*, on the one hand, and (ii) Facebook comments, on the other hand, as if one were also talking about (iii) gender violence in South Africa. Basically, these three – without ever being completely subsumable into one another – turn out to be legitimate and authentic (i) bodies (or forms) of knowledge, (ii) discursive formations, (iii) practices of articulation, and (iv) interpretive terrains. Studying these three elements together opens the way to understanding the social practices and power relations that explain and express gender violence. Indeed, not only has the sharp distinction and a priori separation between "inside" and "outside" fallen away, but one of the methodological conditions that produces them (the one distinguishing between qualitative and quantitative) no longer holds. If Laclau and Mouffe (1985, p. 107) are correct, then there is no necessary ontological difference between "the linguistic and behavioural aspects of a social practice."

In fact, even if *Scandal!* were a "mere" soap opera and Facebook a "mere" social media platform (and thus both heavily immersed in the politics of representation which maintains a distinction between signifier and signified), the discursive approach to social media "talk" allows us to focus on the way in which particular Facebook communities construct their forms of "talk"; their relationship to what they watch and enjoy watching; and their perspectives on the representation of intimate partner violence and gender violence. I was interested in how this community of "talk" is produced (and therefore in its discursive identity), but on the other hand, I was interested in what this very discursive "construction" of this community of *Scandal!* audiences had to say about perceptions about gender violence in the "real world." What we have achieved here is a degree of transcendence of the narrow limits of "outside" and "inside." Hence, the notion of social media "talk" is finally merely the first step in a broadly feminist critique of (i) the representation of gender violence, (ii) perceptions of gender violence, and (iii) gender violence itself. In the end, the whole notion of social media "talk" is always already political.

Each comment, and parts of each comment, express subjectivities and signifying practices that not only enliven our understanding of gender violence, but give it methodological, intellectual, theoretical, and political significance. The concept of "offline" and "online" is key to digital media feminist activism because it gives issues that affect women a voice to be heard and receive attention. This takes us to analysing the #AmINext hashtag which is now an online cultural identity space for GBV victims and supporters in South Africa.

Is #AmINext a rhetoric or real question?

If we take the concept of the "outside" and "inside," we notice that social media platforms such as Twitter have thankfully given agency to many who turn to it to express their anger on social issues. When the hashtag #AmINext was used to campaign against GBV in South Africa in 2019 after Uyinene Mrwetyana, a student from Cape Town University, was raped and murdered, "Am I next?" became a pertinent and valid question. That is the reality "outside" there. Women in South Africa seem to agree that it is a question they ask themselves every day in the face of rising GBV cases, particularly femicide. In the mean time, the life "inside" comprises a digital war on GBV. The #AmINext hashtag stood out from other hashtags such as #EnoughIsEnough and #SAShutdown which ran concurrently when Uyinene was murdered. The #AmINext hashtag was also coming on the back of other hashtags that proved to be powerful forces online in South Africa, such as the #FeesMustFall and #ZumaMustFall campaigns in 2015 and 2017 respectively, which fuelled and fundamentally transformed digital media activism in South Africa. However, studies have shown that there is a tendency for campaigns such as the #AmINext to die down until another high-profile woman is killed. Some wondered whether if Uyinene – raped and murdered at an unusual and public place, the Post Office – had not been a student from Cape Town University, one of South Africa's top universities, the level of outrage and publicity would have been the same. But what seems clear about the digital media activism witnessed on the #AmINext hashtag was how the changing feminist campaigns developed into mass power to demand action, unlike in the past. The "inside," it appears, has a real influence on what is going on "outside."

It is not easy to see why, as at least 330 million use Twitter per month globally, with 500 million Tweets per day (Lin, 2019). In South Africa, there are about 8 million Twitter and 16 million Facebook users. Facebook has "more than three billion people in the world who use the platform to share ideas, offer support, and make a difference" (Facebook, 2020). Facebook helps people to connect among one another and to express themselves, enabling the sharing of at least 100 billion messages and 1 billion stories every day. About 92 per cent of South Africans are believed to be on Facebook during prime time TV from 5 to 9 p.m. (Deep Thought Media, 2020).

Globally, Twitter is increasingly being used to gauge people's feelings or how they are coping with an issue (Wu, 2020). Twitter is "what is happening in the world and what people are "talking about right now" (Stennis, 2018). The feminist digital media activism era has been focusing on areas mainly affecting women, such as rape culture and intersectionality (Rivers, 2017, p. 149; Chamberlain, 2017, p. 3). Digital media activism is a Web-based tool that enables users to share and create content on online platforms to bring about political or social change (Tan, Ponnam, Gillham, Edwards, and Johnson, 2013, p. 1259). Despite a plethora of feminist hashtags in South Africa, studies around them are largely underexplored. The use of digital media by feminists allows them to share anything without having to rely on feminist organisations, in contrast to previous generations. It is through digital media activism that the hashtag phenomenon has grown, and feminists are using it to ignite conversations on issues that affect them.

The #MeToo campaign is a signal case as it was driven purely by social media "talk," the "inside" world. This world has become a feminist cultural identity place, and feminists are using it to contextualise their own issues. The #MeToo campaign is an example of a feminist hashtag that brought out many feminisms from many regions around the globe. Localised hashtags such as #AmINext which mimicked the #MeToo campaign brought out GBV issues that affect marginalised black women, highlighting cases of murders of women who we would not normally hear about. The #MeToo movement has shown that social media "talk" can be an effective tool both for sharing personal narratives and for advocacy in tackling persistent, hidden problems women face. Previously hidden cases of sexual harassment have come to the fore, and women are using social media to refuse to be shut out as before. #MeToo foregrounded sexual harassment, with victims pointing out how the campaign had made them realise how many times they had actually been sexually harassed throughout their lives without noticing it.

Digital media activism represents alternative media where citizens congregate and engage in critical conversations through sharing of lived experiences. Although these spaces are fragmented and segmented, to some audiences they remain the only mainstream public places in which they access information or publish their views. Sadly, as explained in the previous chapter, the digital divide is a concern as it leaves out women in the margins who are not able to participate in social media conversations due to high data costs and lack of access to smartphones. There is also the dilemma of the dichotomy in digital spaces which are viewed as safe due to online anonymity, but are also used as a tool for misogynistic comments.

The "inside" world appears as if it is a place for action to fix the "outside." The #AmINext campaign witnessed massive sharing of information in the form of statistics, petitions, stories, movies, books, photographs, animations and songs, videos, podcasts, and true life GBV examples (Phiri, 2020). For example, there were several calls for protests around GBV on the back of the

#AmINext hashtag. Information was shared in real time, including upcoming protest events both globally and locally, as well as contact details, and in some cases, transport arrangements were offered to take protesters to protest venues. There were calls for collaborative protests and sharing of protest guides (Phiri, 2020). Helping us understand why people share on social media, Courtney Seiter (2016) observes that people view it as an investment that their posts will also be shared and build relationships and a reciprocity effect. This means that social media raises the scope for collaborative work and offers opportunities for deeper connections that may lead to synergies around a particular topic with like-minded organisations and individuals to drive behavioural change, but at the same it provides an opportunity for sisterhood and also for men to participate, as we saw in the previous chapter that feminism has taken on many forms as well as being inclusive of many groups, such as men. Social media platforms bring out voices from varied gender groups that may not identify themselves as women or men.

From a cyberfeminist perspective, digital media feminist activism as witnessed on the #AmINext hashtag is often hyped by other feminist voices and actions. This tells us that social media is being used to promote a feminist culture in ways that were not possible in the past. A example of how #AmINext audiences took advantage of the hashtag was when a South African online media asked South Africans to share their gender-based violence experiences which it was going to publish on its website (news24, 2019). Another example was the initiative by the South African Society of Obstetricians and Gynaecology, which announced on the #AmINext hashtag its introduction of new guidelines that would require the screening of IPV victims as part of the routine medical history (Maphanga, 2019). The organisation said it had been spurred by the social media outcry on #AmINext to change its guidelines because IPV is not easily detectable since it takes place in the privacy of homes. The guidelines would require health practitioners to identify signs of abuse and offer support and treatment.

Both the digital media activism we saw on the #AmINext hashtag and *Scandal!*'s Facebook posts protesting about the violence against Gloria by Obakeng had several similarities. For example, even though *Scandal!* is a soap opera and not real life, the Facebook audiences reacted angrily to Gloria, a Township woman, for not taking swift action to end her marriage when she began to be abused by her husband, Obakeng. This opens up the issue of how Black marginalised women address GBV. The participants of the Facebook "talk" were so proactively "feminist" in their discourse that they used their "advice" to compel the producers of *Scandal!* to implement the Facebook audience's frantic suggestions to let Gloria finally "walk away" and file a divorce to create a "safe" ending. *Scandal!* contends this was coincidental because the episodes are prepared three months before television viewing and are written four months ahead, so audiences could not have influenced the ending of the storyline. According to *Scandal!*, the reality is that audiences wanted different outcomes such as a "happily ever after" ending with a husband, wife, and children and no violence. The ending with the arrest of Obakeng was unexpected, and some audiences did not like it (Mahlaba, 2023).

Due to digital media feminist activism, we see that Obakeng was ultimately sent to jail as a result of such "suggestions." The producers of *Scandal!* were also "advised" to find Gloria another man. Although he was a fictitious character, Obakeng was called a "bastard," "dog," "controller," "not man enough," "pig," "experienced abuser who gets away with it," "bull," "woman beater," "pervert," "monster," "coward," "ugly," "insecure," "stupid," "rat," "shameless," "jealous mamma's boy," "good for nothing," "fool," and "pervert." This included violent calls to "meet him for advice" and to castrate him and feed his private parts to dogs. This name-calling we saw on Facebook regarding *Scandal!* was similar to the audience responses in the #AmINext Twitter hashtag, where men were branded rapists. Some commenters claimed that some men lost their jobs as some companies dismissed workers who had been named and shamed on the #AmINext hashtag (Phiri, 2020). In a clear demonstration of the intolerance of GBV, some companies posted that they had fired their employees and would not let them undertake any future work with them after their names were called out on #AmINext. Other men called out on the same platform alleged that they had received death threats, and reported the loss of major business contracts. The name-calling touched on government officials, politicians, and celebrities, triggering controversy, with some social media audiences questioning whether the finger pointing was ethical. One post warned that while naming and shaming was an effective form of retribution, particularly if the posters could prove the allegations, it accused women of using the #AmINext hashtag to settle old scores and being defamatory. One man who had been named and shamed published a statement rebutting the allegations and stating he would sue his accuser and former lover. Another poster published an apology to the man she had named and shamed.

This type of digital media activism in the "inside" produced offline action on the "outside" that would have been impossible to mobilise without social media platforms. This kind of activism is different from the feminist movement of the past, which relied mostly on advocacy and lobbying strategies to push governments to adopt laws and international instruments. Often these are hard to enforce or implement, sometimes due to cultural or attitudinal barriers. Some studies in South Africa have suggested that court outcomes "insult or ridicule" the laws rather than respect and abide by them (Mogale et al., 2012). Essentially, it is thought that the courts are not doing enough to uphold the law or to show the way in terms of how to end the epidemic of violence against women. The unfriendly attitude of police towards victims of IPV and the corrupt judicial system that lets perpetrators of IPV walk free or causes police dockets to disappear are among other challenges. This reveals how feminism is still relevant, contrary to views that human rights violations such as GBV can only be fought using the justice system. Studies have recommended novel interventions that may help to curb violence against women *apart from* what the slow-moving wheels of the courts can do. Such interventions include considering the granular and ineffable nature of violence against women, particularly in everyday contexts and spaces. Digital media activism is an "inside" tool that is part of a broader feminist politics, helping to shape the voices of women to keep the GBV matter on South Africa's agenda both politically and in the media. Pre-social media feminist movements also relied on mobilising women's movements, for advocacy and lobbying of friendly laws, although most often these organisations had no capacity to reach women in the same way digital media currently does. The "inside" forces seem to have more power than the "outside" in the social media era. Feminism, as we saw in Chapter 3, is in some African cultures misunderstood and considered foreign and Western, but with digital media activism, feminism has taken a new turn because people have an opportunity to share their voices freely without fear of being labelled. However, the clicktivism era has sought to change how feminist ideas spread, and the next section argues that merely clicking on social media is an act of social resistance.

Clicktivism: social resistance or waste of time?

Many digitally connected Millennials and subsequent generations cannot imagine a world without social media or search engines. The sharing of comments about GBV on the #AmINext hashtag or the etvScandal Facebook page can be viewed as "slacktivism or clicktivism" (Morozov, 2009). Morozov coined the terms "slacktivism" and "clicktivism" – feel-good activism where there is no social impact. However, this book argues that slacktivism or clicktivism on its own is necessary as it is a form of resistance. This is because even if feminist digital media activism does not result in physical revolution, the conversations it generates partly influence a feminist identity culture which we have seen building up with the rise of the #MeToo and #BlackLivesMatter movements. For example, the #MeToo movement resulted in more than 200 powerful men losing their jobs in the USA within a year of the movement's founding (El-Faizy, 2021).

In South Africa, #AmINext and campaigns such as those run by *Scandal!* are helping to break the patriarchal boundaries that silence women and challenge toxic masculinity that results in GBV, contributing to legislation changes, also emphasising the power of the "inside" world. There have been statutory prohibitions against committing violence against women, as expressed in two signal pieces of South African legislation, the Domestic Violence Act No 116 of 1998 and the Criminal Law Sexual Offences and Related Matters Act No 32 of 2007, but in 2022 South Africa introduced three new pieces of legislation to deal with alarming cases of GBV. The Criminal Law (Sexual Offences and Related Matters) Amendment Bill, the Criminal and Related Matters Amendment Bill, and the Domestic

Violence Amendment Bill were first introduced in the country's parliament in 2020 following a public outcry for the government to take GBV cases seriously, particularly after the rape and murder of Uyinene (Mlaba, 2022). Under the laws, sexual offenders will be listed on a national register, and they will make accessing protection orders easier by enabling victims to apply online. The new laws also redefine domestic violence to extend to victims of assault among those engaged to be married, dating, in customary relationships, and those in actual or perceived romantic, intimate, or sexual relationships of any duration.

While the "inside" world has power to influence the world out there, such as pushing for friendly laws against GBV, barriers continue to affect the "outside" in terms of how people talk about what affects them. Concerns have also been raised about the GBV narrative which talks about how many women are raped as opposed to how many men have committed rape. The suggestion is that such a narrative takes the focus off men and shifts it onto women. This point reveals how feminism is relevant and is used to draw conclusions. The term "violence against women" is also problematic because it suggests nobody is perpetrating violence on the women, it just happens. Supporting these sentiments are those who suggest that calling it gender-based violence is running away from naming what it is. The truth is that it is the "murder and beating up of women by men in South Africa," according to Songezo Zibi (2014, p. 240), who has written on gender equality in his book *Raising the Bar: Hope and Renewal in South Africa*. Love (2019) applauds the kind of digital media activism we see in #AmINext as something that puts women's experiences at the centre. For example, the murder of Uyinene was followed by posts of other cases of rape and femicide in South Africa.

South Africa's #AmINext hashtag is not the first feminist hashtag rage against GBV witnessed in the world. #AmINext originated in Canada, where it has been in use since 2014 when a student, Lorreta Saunders, was murdered just before her graduation, and ironically, she had been working on a thesis on missing and murdered Indigenous women (Thomson, 2014). Her Canadian cousin, Holly Jarret, initiated the #AmINext hashtag to highlight the high rate of missing and murdered of indigenous Canadian women by raising awareness and encouraging national dialogue through the controversial hashtag after the murder of Saunders and that of other women killed soon after. It was controversial because in her campaign Saunders asked people to take photos of themselves holding the sign #AmINext, and the public questioned "the long-term value of posting a video or photo of yourself online" (Thomson, 2014). Both in Canada and in the analysis of South Africa's #AmINext hashtag, some people also questioned whether the question "Am I next?" was self-defeating to women, instilling fear as well as removing the focus from the actual victims to potential victims. These varied views are part of postmodern feminism where there is simply no one truth.

Where next for social media activism?

As Wu (2020) points out, social media data provides "a clearer picture" of what to expect from people. The fear of being the next potential victim of IPV-motivated murder stoked anger and influenced Twitter audiences of the #AmINext hashtag to initiate two petitions through change.org. One called for the death penalty for crimes against women, and the other called for GBV to be declared a state of emergency. By June 2020, exactly ten months after the two petitions were shared on #AmINext on social media, they had been signed by more than 670,000 and 630,000 people respectively out of the combined target of 2 million people (Agent of Change, 2019; Gillion, 2019). South Africa abolished the death penalty in 1995 on the grounds that it "contravenes the Constitution, violating the right to life, dignity and freedom and security of a person" (Weiner, 2019). Weiner postulates that brutality for brutality is not a solution. Calls to bring back the death penalty may be signs that women in South Africa have had enough, so the question is: where to from here?

There are always issues that threaten progress made on platforms such as #AmINext. Zibi (2014, p. 240) insists that if toxic masculinity is not tackled, the issue of gender-based violence will remain problematic. Toxic masculinity is defined as a constellation of social attitudes that define masculine gender in terms of violence, sexual aggression, and lack of emotional expressions, and is thought to be directly linked to gender-based violence (Hoffmeester, 2017). Chapter 1 raised the issue of manosphere, which contributes to toxic masculinity. This type of masculinity consists of norms, behaviours, and beliefs which lead to sexism, misogyny, aggression, the glorification of violence, and the "sexual objectification of women" (Sculos, 2017). It devalues women, conveys homophobic behaviours, and fosters domination. Zibi (2014, p. 240) says such a culture of violence in South Africa makes it difficult for men to respect women. #AmINext is thus not a protest, but a revolution that signifies taking a stand. It is thus not a trend or joke if women are being killed daily, but an outcry for men to stop trivialising the plight of women due to patriarchal values which give some men a sense of entitlement. In *Scandal!*, we see this sense of entitlement when Obakeng shames Gloria, for instance, for not carrying out household chores and doing her "wifely duties" such as cooking for him. This is an attempt to inscribe her body as good only for domestication and for gratification of male needs. Gloria, however, has desires that exceed the space of the kitchen. This leads to conflict between husband and wife. Meanwhile, Obakeng does not see any contradiction in his travelling on work assignments and enjoying the freedom that comes with such travel. It is as if men are naturally made for public spaces and the broader public realm.

Digital media activism appears to be the new coping mechanism culture for women. I noticed that both *Scandal!*'s Facebook campaign against GBV and the #AmINext hashtag on Twitter platform have become more like extensions of homes where audiences share intimate personal stories, including practical help and advice about abusive partners. Real safety tips like the use of pepper sprays, tracking apps, self-defence courses, use of female-driven car ride apps, where to find healing, and the utilisation of WhatsApp live location pins when feeling at risk were among those shared. Warnings were issued on Twitter about men considered dangerous to women and cars to watch out for, including unsafe roads and routes.

In both campaigns, commenters from other countries in the region talked about how GBV was affecting their countries too – a sign that it is not an isolated problem. The "inside" informs us what is going on in other worlds "outside." It also reveals how the feminist ideology as it relates to GBV is shared across many African countries. Digital media activism is thus a unifier for feminists who are against GBV. One conversation thread on the #AmINext hashtag had people talking about GBV in Malawi and how the country had tackled the problem by raising the marriage age from 16 to 18 years, establishing victim support units, ratifying international conventions, establishing mobile courts, and setting up GBV hotlines. A commenter from Namibia mentioned how the country faced challenges in the implementation of GBV laws and instruments as well as the lack of coordination among key service providers, high levels of withdrawal of GBV cases by the survivors, and the lack of GBV referral mechanisms. Other examples were drawn from Tanzania, Zambia, Zimbabwe, Nigeria, and the experiences of the Southern Africa Development Community, which was apparently working on a model law. A similar trend emerged on the *Scandal!* Facebook page as well, where viewers from the region also shared their experiences, helping to expose GBV in other African countries. There were thus forums to learn and share from others as well as show the gaps that exist. The feminist ideas from these countries showed that while there were different ways of tackling GBV, there was a common purpose to stop the oppression.

There is no doubt that the digital media activism described in this book helps us gain an understanding of the meaning and experience dimensions of humans' lives and social worlds.[1] Chapter 5 will take us on a tour of the nature of "talk," the significance of language as a tool and ammunition that can be used to fight GBV, and the concept of feminist digital political activism.

Note

1 Fossey, E., Harvey, C., McDermott, F., & Davidson, L. (2002) "Understanding and evaluating qualitative research", *Australian and New Zealand Journal of Psychiatry*, 36: 717–732.

References

Agent of Change. (2019). Bring back the death sentence in SA for crimes against women. Home page. https://www.change.org/p/south-african-government-bring-back-the-death-sentence-in-sa-for-crimes-against-women.

Chamberlain, P. (2017). *The feminist fourth wave: Affective temporality*. London: Springer Nature. https://doi.org/10.1007/978-3-319-53682-8.

Deep Thought Media. (2020). Facebook statistics South Africa. Deep Thought Media. Home page. https://deepthoughtmedia.co.za/article/facebook-statistics-south-africa/. Accessed 2021/12/02.

El-Faizzy, M. (2021). After a sluggish start, #Metoo movements pick up steam in France. 17/02/2021. Home page. https://amp.france24.com/en/france/20210217-after-a-sluggish-start-metoo-movements-pick-up-steam-france.

Facebook. (2020). Our mission: Give people the power to build the community and bring the world closer together. Facebook. https://about.fb.com/company-info/.

Gillion, L. (2019). Parliament needs to address gender-based violence in South Africa. Change.org. https://bit.ly/37KmNs2/.

Hoffmeester, D. (2017, June 29). Masculinity in crisis. Institute for Justice and Reconcilliation. https://www.ijr.org.za/2017/06/29/masculinity-in-crisis/.

Kozinets, R.V. (2010). *Netnography: Doing ethnographic research online*. London: Sage.

Kozinets, R.V. (2015). *Netnography redefined* (Second Edition). London: Sage Publications.

Laclau, E., & Mouffe, C. (1985). *Hegemony and socialist strategy: Towards a radical democratic politics*. London: Verso.

Lin, Y. (2019). Twitter statistics every marketer should know in 2020. https://bit.ly/3htiNAB/. 2020/11/10.

Love, A. (2019). Digital Black feminism. In Parry, D., Johnson, C., Fullagar, S. (Eds), *Digital Dilemmas*. Cham: Palgrave Macmillan. https://doi.org/10.1007/978-3-319-95300-7_3 the feminist movement is traditionally ignored, marginalised, and ridiculed.

Mahlaba, G. (2023). WhatsApp interview. Johannesburg. February. Interview notes available from the author.

Mlaba, K. (2022, February 1). South Africa just adopted new laws on gender-based violence: Here's what to know. Home page. https://www.globalcitizen.org/en/content/south-africa-adopts-three-new-gbv-laws/?utm_source=Iterable&utm_medium=email&utm_campaign=SA_2022-02-04_Content_Digest. Accessed 2022/05/16.

Maphanga, C. (2019). #AmINext: New screening guidelines for gynaecologists, obstetricians. news24. Home page. https://www.news24.com/news24/southafrica/news/aminext-new-screening-guidelines-for-gynaecologists-obstetricians-20190910/. Accessed 2020/07/16.

Mogale, S.R., Barns, K.K., & Ritcher, S. (2012). Violence against women in South Africa: Policy position and recommendations. *Violence against Women*, 18(5), 580–594.

Morozov, E. (2009). The brave new world of slacktivism. Home page. https://foreignpolicy.com/2009/05/19/the-brave-new-world-of-slacktivism/. Accessed 2021/02/28.

news24 (2019). AmINext: news24 wants to give you a platform to share your feelings with the nation. News24. https://www.news24.com/news24/southafrica/news/aminext-news24-wants-to-give-you-a-platform-to-share-your-feelings-with-the-nation-20190905/. Accessed 2020/09/05.

Phiri, M. (2020). *Facebook and Twitter- A feminist digital narrative of gender-based violence*. Unpublished paper.

Phiri, M. (2021). Coronavirus Satire: A dissection of feminist politics and humour. In Mpofu, S. (Ed), *Digital humour in the Covid-19 pandemic: Perspectives from the Global South*. Cham: Palgrave MacMillan, pp. 167–189.

Rivers, N. (2017). *Post feminism (s) and the arrival of the fourth wave: Turning tides*. Cham, London: Palgrave Macmillan .

Sayyid, B., & Zac, L. (1998). Political analysis in a world without foundations. In Scarbrough, E., & Tanenbaum, E. (Eds), *Research strategies in the social sciences*. Oxford: Oxford University Press, pp. 249–267.

Seiter, C. (2016). The Psychology of social media: Why we like, comment, and share online. *Buffer*. https://buffer.com/resources/psychology-of-social-media/. Accessed 2016/08/10.

Stennis, C. (2018). Defining what makes Twitter audience unique. Blog.twitter.com. https://blog.twitter.com/en_us/topics/insights/2018/defining-what-makes-twitters-audience-unique.html/.

Sculos, B.W. (2017). Who's afraid of 'toxic masculinity'? *Class, Race and Corporate Power*, 5(3), 1–5. DOI: 10.25148/CRCP.5.3.006517 Available at: https://digitalcommons.fiu.edu/classracecorporatepower/vol5/iss3/6

Tan, L., Ponnam, S., Gillham, P., Edwards, B., & Johnson, E. (2013, August). Analyzing the impact of social media on social movements: A computational study on Twitter and the occupy wall street movement. In Proceedings of the 2013 IEEE/ACM International Conference on Advances in Social Networks Analysis and Mining (pp. 1259–1266). https://scholar.google.com/scholar?hl=en&as_sdt=0%2C5&q=Tan%2C+Ponnam&btnG=

Thomson, A. (2014, September, 13). #AmINext aims to raise awareness about murdered Aboriginal women. CBC. Nova Scotia. https://bit.ly/3foIYXj/.

Weiner, J. (2019). Bringing back the death penalty in South Africa for crimes against women. Oxford Human rights hub. Home page. https://ohrh.law.ox.ac.uk/bringing-back-the-death-penalty-in-south-africa-for-crimes-against-women/. Accessed 2019/10/01.

Wu, K. (2020). With social data, brands have a clearer picture of what customers expect and need in the time of COVID-19. blog.twitter.com. Home page. https://blog.twitter.com/en_us/topics/insights/2020/why-social-data-is-key-for-brands-in-COVID-19.html/. Accessed 2020/05/14.

Zibi, S. (2014). *Raising the bar: Hope and renewal in South Africa*. London: Picardo Africa.

5 The nature of GBV social media "talk," language, audiences

Introduction

Digital media activism certainly enhances awareness of previously ignored issues considered taboo subjects. People, including feminist groups and ordinary women, use it to instigate "talk" that allows people to express themselves in a way they would not have done in the past. The findings in relation to how social media audiences chatted and talked about gender violence related specifically to a few "awarenesses," such as the awareness of the complex nature of gender violence, awareness of Obakeng as an abusive partner, awareness of stages of abuse, awareness of the nature of violence and control, awareness of "representation tensions," and awareness of Gloria's predicament, and of Gloria as the victim of abuse.

This book re-defines feminist praxis surrounding not only gender violence, but related issues such as marriage, inheritance, and misogyny. Subjecting this "talk" to the blended feminist theory helped to see how people talk about GBV from a woman's focal point and how this online talk morphs into offline actions that are also women-centred. The feminist part of this activism may not have been easy to detect without subjecting it to rigorous feminist thinking, as this book does. For example, from the analysis, it is apparent that audiences could certainly see the profile of an abusive partner in Obakeng, and how awareness of masculinity and patriarchy was evident in the social media "talk." It was clear that audiences were aware of the multiform nature of gender violence; they had an awareness of the different types of intimate partner violence, and were also aware of the nature of the abusive personality.

Analysis of this "talk" helped to establish that both *Scandal!* and the #AmINext hashtag provided a platform for venting, education, counselling, and sharing of experiences of abuse and murders of women in townships and informal settlements. They were also platforms for sharing of information about missing women and girls from marginalised communities suspected of being murdered or those living in abusive relationships but finding it hard to get out. Bringing out cases of marginalised women's experiences was critical information that we would not ordinarily learn about without using a feminist lens to examine this kind of digital media activism. This was key, because

DOI: 10.4324/9781003260820-5

it is rare for online feminist experiences and knowledge about GBV to be documented in books.

We learn from this type of digital media feminist activism that there was a general awareness in the forums of the *psychological* behaviour of men who abuse women. In Facebook's etvScandal "talk," there was a clear awareness of Obakeng as an abuser. For example, it was clear in the comments that there was consciousness that "abusive men shift blame and don't realise they have a problem." As some of the participants in the social media "talk" put it, "they make you feel guilty," they "hit you again and again," and they "hit you then apologise."

Sifting out these comments was a key learning curve for those experiencing gender violence directly or indirectly. The awareness of Obakeng as an abuser and the real murders of women posted on the #AmINext hashtag were reflected in the angry epithets and extensive name-calling directed at men who had killed women. Without subjecting this to a feminist analysis, this anger may not have made sense. As shown in the previous chapter, the #AmINext campaign was rife with name-calling and men-shaming, leading to loss of jobs, with some threatened with police or court action. Name-calling and trolling are practices that are amplified on social media. It is well nigh impossible to find social media threads where there is no trolling and name-calling. Research has shown that this is partly facilitated by online anonymity (cf. Kozinets, 2015). From a cyberfeminist view, it is refreshing to note that other participants noticed and expressed anger by stating that Obakeng annoyed and disgusted them, that he "sucks," and so on, which was a clear statement that violence against women is shunned even though statistics are alarming. Phrases such as "I don't like him," "I will kill him," and "he must burn in hell" were frequently used on both etvScandal and the #AmINext hashtag. There were even veiled threats, such as "I want to meet with him for advice," on the etvScandal Facebook page, referring to Obakeng's abuse. This is a sign that digital media feminist activism is not simply clicktivism, but is often accompanied by the desire for offline solutions. It makes this kind of feminism more powerful, nuanced, and focused as it is driven mostly by people, and furthermore, it influences policy makers to act, such as by passing laws.

Gloria was not spared from the angry comments and name-calling either. Audiences felt she was being negatively stereotyped. Black feminism has always been concerned at the way Black women are represented in the media and how it perpetuates stereotypes that keep women overlooked. I noted that there was much frustration at Gloria's own ambivalent behaviour and the sense that she was a "weak victim." Gloria's ambivalence and "split personality" (she is seen as dithering and as not knowing what she really wants) left many of the commenters "split." The "weakening" of Gloria was noted by most commenters, and was attributed to the efforts of the producers of *Scandal!* to try to create a character who could be bullied and abused to show how bad gender violence was. This strategy, however, was regarded as reinforcing the stereotype that Black women are not assertive, and are weak, passive, and yield to power. Ayiera (2010, p. 12) fears such a "categorisation normalises the notion of women lacking agency and in need of protection." The problem with stereotypes is, as Black feminist Chimamanda Ngozi Adichie (2009) succinctly points out: "Show a people as one thing over and over again and that is what they become." Many wondered why Gloria did not leave or act decisively against Obakeng early on. As observed earlier, some of the audiences tended to blame the victim. For others, it seemed to be a case of frustration with the dithering and paralysis of the character. When she starts dating Obakeng, the usual Gloria who is strong-willed disappears, to be replaced by a timid, weak, and voiceless "impostor." This impostor role is so topical that it dominates a large section of the entire "talk." Some of the commenters who were critical of the "weak" Gloria stated the following:

- "Gloria is sending a bad message to women who are being abused."
- "Gloria is a bad example to women ...."
- "Gloria enjoys being abused, she deserves to be abused, why defend someone abusing you?"
- "What an example are you setting for your children?"

Audiences wanted to know what happened to the Gloria they knew, and why she was portrayed as a victim for a protracted length of time before her triumphant ending. Indeed, many confessed that they could not reconcile the two personalities. How could such a strong personality be so weak? Some commenters wished Gloria would be much more decisive, but as *Scandal!* clarifies, Gloria was mirroring what happens in society. Such readings by the audiences tended towards a discrepant decoding, where audiences saw meanings that were contrary to those encoded by the producers of the messages. As Mann (2014) observes, new media has become a site of struggle over meaning, representation, and participation. I observed the morphing and merging of the "inside" of the soap opera and the "outside" of the real world when some commenters spoke about their own real-world experiences that were being mirrored by the drama between Gloria and Obakeng.

Digital media feminist activism reveals the complexity of GBV. Audiences could not understand what was behind the passive acceptance of abuse. Considering the fragmentary nature of social media "talk," how informed was the "debate" on the subject as a whole? Gloria was labelled a "fool," "dumb," "stupid," "desperate," "weak," "blind," "a bad example to women," "loser," and "boring." Some were angry with her because they felt that she enjoyed the abuse. She was accused of being blind to her situation. Much unsolicited "advice" was offered to her. For instance, some suggested solutions that were problematic, such as wishing Gloria could go back to her first husband. Abel, as noted earlier, had cheated on her, and had already married another woman. This is because divorced and single women in the Black cultures are often stigmatised. Issues of independence and sexuality of single women are hardly talked about. Phiri (2021) notes that traditionally, single divorced women in southern African countries are stigmatised and often blamed for marriage breakdowns, and for a variety of reasons such as miscarriages, failure to bear children, failure to satisfy the man in bed, lack of cooking skills, not able to perform household chores to the satisfaction of their men, and failure to treat the husband's relatives well because when a woman is married, she marries her whole husband's community. While there is a lot of focus on single women, the single status of men is largely uncontested unless it is in the context of post-divorce or mid-life crisis. Singleness is frowned upon among the Black culture, where marriage is associated with stability, but social media is helping to de-mythicise such cultural beliefs. Being single and having sexual independence is synonymous with being a "slut" (Chambers, 2005, p. 171).

As noted, this "participation" by the audience in the GBV conversation constitutes part of the tapestry of social television that has now been made possible by social media. As reality shows such as *Idol*, *The Voice*, and *Big Brother* have shown, audience participation is possible through comments and voting. The traditional idea of television as just a one-way flow is no longer tenable. The diversity of comments exemplifies this two-way interaction, as shown by the fact that, while there was a general feeling of anger and disgust towards Obakeng for being a serial abuser and seemingly getting away with it, there was also negativity towards Gloria for allowing the abuse to happen for too long before realising her predicament. They were concerned with why Gloria would not press charges, why she did not say "enough is enough" and seek help immediately. They were worried about why it was not easy for her to break her silence on the violence perpetrated on her by her second husband, Obakeng.

Audiences did show an awareness of the complexity of domestic abuse among Black township women like Gloria. Gloria's name was mentioned a total of 215 times in the threads, while that of Obakeng was mentioned 105 times. However, other commenters related to Gloria's "split personality" and to the "dithering" and paralysed behaviour, saying that it is not always so easy to "get out." Others also reminded their interlocutors that violence against women was a complex issue that defied straightforward answers. At any rate, soap operas need not necessarily proceed according to laws of chronological unfolding that we perhaps see in our daily lives. It could also be contended that the idea to portray Gloria as weak could have been merely to mirror the reality of what goes on in many South African Black homes. Perhaps this is what, from a point of view of representation, Porter (1977) observed as the function of soap operas: "solutions to the problems posed by soap operas are of such a kind that they are themselves generative of further problems."

It is possible that Gloria is genuinely paralysed and trapped by the abuse, such that she is unable to get out. As one commenter on a thread stated, "abusers hit you again and again then apologise." Acknowledging the repetitive and cyclic peaks and troughs of abuse is important: the abuse gets worse incrementally, and sometimes it is too late. Note that Gloria only "notices" that she is a victim of abuse when the violence becomes physical. Before that, the immediate tendency is for the woman to rationalise the abuse or to blame herself. A commenter put it succinctly when she stated that "Obakeng wants Gloria to feel it's her fault when he beat her." The general attitude towards Gloria at times seemed to me to reflect a tendency to blame the victim, or to blame the producers for watering down Gloria's character to make a point. Some commenters, for instance, speculated about the extent to which Gloria provoked her husband. For instance, some commenters accused Gloria of acting like a "prostitute" by holding tripe nights and flirting with other men even though she was a married woman. Some thought she provoked and "pushed" Obakeng to beat her up, or that she asked for it. Hence comments such as "I understand where he is coming from." But should there be an excuse for abuse? Feminist critiques unanimously show that the abuser is the only person solely responsible for the abuse and the only one who can stop it. A feminist-lite comment is thus seen in the retort: "You can never ask to be hit" and "there is no excuse of beating a woman."

The final issue in terms of awareness concerns whether audiences were aware of Gloria's role as a victim and their understanding of (the toll of) trauma and survival. The audience was aware of the double consciousness that Gloria had to develop to pretend that all was well, and the fear of communal backlash for outing Obakeng as an abuser. Exasperated posts expressed the view that it was "typical of women" to not quickly move out and away from an abuser. Indeed, some commenters felt like "clapping" Gloria, just to help her to "wake up" to the reality that being beaten does not constitute love. As such, the threats of violence were not targeted only at Obakeng, but also at the victim. As noted, such threats also show the thin line between "inside" and "outside," online and offline. Still others counselled that unless one is in Gloria's shoes, one can never know how it feels to be in such a situation in real life.

Of critical importance was that the comments exhibited zero tolerance for violence against women on both the *Scandal!* show and the #AmINext hashtag. The abuse of women was regarded as a "no-no." There was no open support, for instance, for Obakeng's actions, particularly when his actions escalated to physical violence. Obakeng came out clearly as the pantomime villain in most of the comments. Such a reading would be a form of preferred or dominant decoding, since this is also the reading of Obakeng that is consistent with the needs of *Scandal!*'s producers as far as the 16 Days of Activism are concerned. Although not calling it feminism, the producers took a feminist political decision that certainly wanted Obakeng to be seen unambiguously as the aggressor and Gloria as the victim. They also wanted audiences to condemn domestic abuse directly. These outcomes were by and large realised simply because the producers had taken a subtle feminist-centric stance aimed at helping to eradicate GBV. Analysing GBV from a feminist position also helped to bring out the injustices of GBV. As Geraghty (2001, p. 17) argues, soap operas provide stories which engage an audience in such a way that the stories become the "subject for public interest and interrogation," and in this case, it was GBV. The direction and flow of "talk" focused on domestic violence by men against women, since the *Scandal!* episodes in question were themselves intended to present a picture in which men committed violence against women, and not the other way round. By putting a spotlight on violence against women, *Scandal!* prioritised and made the "feminist position" (or at least the UN gender rights position) a central rallying point. This is a huge difference from the days when soap operas positioned women only as objects of the male gaze.

As noted in Chapter 1, South Africa experiences exceptionally high cases of violence against women (Abrahams et al., 2013). Tshepo Mosese, an actor on *Scandal!*, stated in 2015 that his favourite storyline of the past decade was the one about Gloria and Obakeng:

> My favourite storyline would have to be of Gloria and Obakeng which tackled gender violence. I felt like it was the most relevant story in terms of what is happening in our society today. There are so many women that are from abusive homes. Those stories need to be told. I think that's the one story that is really going to hit home given the fact that so many women are going through that type of situation.[1]

Many commenters on the threads stated that they related to the topic because they had either experienced domestic violence directly or knew a woman or women who had suffered it. The sentiments were the same on the #AmINext hashtag too. In some sense, the fictitious became reality as it mirrored the experiences of the Facebook audience. In this other sense, the Facebook platform was a space of conversation and dialogue. I noticed that whether it was #AmINext discussing Uyinene's murder or the etvScandal Facebook page chats on Gloria, digital media activism is often influenced by what is currently going on. While Uyinene's conversations reflected real-life murders of real people and Gloria's was a fictional character, they were all driven by anger and despair about other murders of women that were being reported on social media. Reeva Steenkamp, Jayde Panayiotou, Fatima Patel, Anni Dewani, Zanele Khumalo, and Dolly Tshabalala were some of the women who made headlines in South Africa in 2014–2015 having been killed by their partners. There is little doubt that these murders resonated widely in South Africa. The clearest indication of this direction and flow of "talk" comes once again from the fact that none of the "talk" referred to domestic violence by women against men. As noted, the *Scandal!* episodes in question were intended to present a picture in which men committed violence against women, and not the other way round.

In terms of the content of the chat or "talk" itself, the soap opera and the social media platform together became a sort of launch pad for the contestation of traditional and feminist ideas on marriage and relationships, with a focus on the two main characters. As noted, the name of the main female character, Gloria, was mentioned 215 times in the threads while that of her abuser, Obakeng, was mentioned 105 times. The word "women" was, however, mentioned less than the word "men," as illustrated in Figure 5.1.

Digital media feminist activism confirms that the way women are framed, positioned, and constructed in traditional media has always been problematic due to power relations and the male gaze which inserts women into media as second-class citizens. The situation is even starker for Black women. Thus representation, in as far as it is regarded as a political issue (Robinson and Richardson, 1997, p. 125), forms a crucial part of the feminist standpoint. Robinson and Richardson posit that without power and agency to define their image and participate in decisions that affect how women are defined, others will be left to decide what makes digital media feminist activism significant. The way women are perceived is influenced in part by the images that are constructed by media such as television – in this case, through the genre of soap opera. Representation is thus a key way in which gendered "reality" is constructed. The grammar we use to "talk" about women is often a reflection of patriarchy (Ayiera, 2010, p. 13). As Dobash and Dobash (1977, p. 1998) explain, we cannot understand partner abuse within contemporary society unless we "understand and recognize the centuries-old legacy of women as

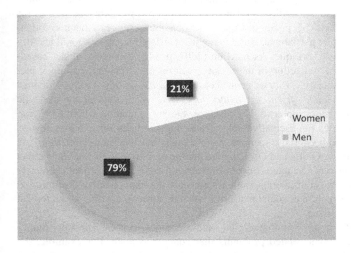

Figure 5.1 The frequency of mentioning the words "men" and "women"

the victims of patriarchal cultures that dominate and control them." Digital media feminist activism is part of this process of learning, understanding, and redefining feminist trajectories.

But if television representations reinforce dominant ideologies, then feminism not only positions itself as the binary opposite of patriarchy/masculinist worldviews of Obakeng, but chips away at this accumulated power. This political and transformative dimension of feminism may be the reason, in Adichie's (2014) words, we must all become feminists. Digital media feminist activism is breaking boundaries and barriers that have prohibited some voices being heard. It was impossible to know the gender of those sharing the comments analysed in this book. Power relations which subordinate women present themselves differently in different cultures. However, feminism identifies the critique of patriarchy and masculinity as central to any project to defeat gender violence. Many commenters on the threads tended to associate Obakeng's abuse with a manifestation of patriarchy. This was reflected, for instance, in some of the epithets and name-calling directed at Obakeng, such as calling him a "bull." The bull is the manifestation of masculinity *par excellence*. As a symbol, it expresses the display of blind male machismo and masculine virility. Bulls do not notice or care when they hurt females, but justify it as being part of their nature. What else is a bull for if not to dominate "his" wives?

Feminists seem to think that men tend to minimise their violent behaviour because of the advantageous position they hold in the structure of gender relations. Certainly, some traditional hierarchies place men in superior positions in relation to women, and some even treat women as personal possessions. Certainly, Obakeng's attempts to domesticate Gloria by limiting her independence and her ability to raise money through tripe nights, as well as his discomfort with her position as the owner of a house, suggests that his motivations might be patriarchal. But it is not just patriarchy that we should identify as the focus of critique. As Joachim (2007, p. 118) contends, gender-based-violence is a "reflection of the broad structures of sexual and economic inequality in society." This was corroborated by a 2017 study, *Violence against women in South Africa: A Country in Crisis*, which showed the systemic nature of gender violence. For instance, the very situation where Obakeng, a senior sales representative selling cleaning products for a big company, is paired with Gloria, a mere cleaner, invokes lopsided power relations. As noted earlier, Gloria and Obakeng are not the main stars of *Scandal*! The fact that a degree of sustained conversation about these relatively minor characters was possible is thus a remarkable testament to the importance of the topic and the "open" nature of social platforms when it comes to chatting about topical or trending issues.

What we learn is that digital media activism presents an opportunity to discuss other related problems that concern women. For example, the etvScandal Facebook comments did not just touch on the Gloria/Obakeng storyline, but included other narratives which were running concurrently with the episodes portraying violence against Gloria. The conversations oscillated between these storylines, although this study confined itself to the narrative about Gloria's abuse. Other storylines on *Scandal!* also depicted some violence against women, albeit not similar to what Gloria was facing. One woman was being victimised and tormented by her husband's half-brother, who seemed to have been going through psychological issues resulting from his violent upbringing. Another was portrayed as a psychopath because she mercilessly manipulated her husband, using lies, cheating, and plotting murder as some of her tactics. The other was a jailbird and dysfunctional mother fighting for her release from prison. Yet another was a young mother who had just given up her baby for adoption and faced alienation from her family. This young mother's only concern, however, was to marry a rich man.

It also emerged that the *etvScandal* Facebook page and the #AmINext hashtag served as educational forums and public spheres for spreading ideologies such as feminist thinking. Habermas defines the notion of public as "when it's open to all" (Fuchs, 2017, p. 218). He therefore sees the important dimensions of the public sphere as formation of public opinion where all citizens have access and thus have freedoms, among them freedom of expression (Haberman, 1989b, p. 136). However, one criticism of this concept is that it ignores the fact that not everyone has access, which is true, as access to Facebook is limited according to internet connectivity and accepting Facebook's controversial Terms and Conditions and Privacy Policy. From a cyberfeminist point of view, the public sphere, according to Fuchs (2017, p. 219), "has been a sphere of educated, rich men whereas the private sphere is viewed as the domain of women," as we will discuss later. Despite the weaknesses, this book reveals that social media is somewhat a public sphere. The attitude that women's lives, just like men's, matter and are important (Reinharz, 1992) was clearly expressed. What emerged, therefore, was a tendency to "talk" repeatedly about violence in relation to gender. Abstract references to "men" and "women" were in abundance. This, I would argue, shows that social media "talk" can be explicitly gendered, just as much as it can be racialised or reflect class or ethnicity. It is probable that it was mainly women watching and commenting about Gloria – at least, the literature suggests that soap opera audiences are still predominantly female (Brunsdon, 2000, p. 29; Mahlaba, 2023). Certainly, there is evidence of emerging identity politics on social media. Such identity politics are heavily inflected as online identities, although with indications that audiences also constantly enrich online threads by referring to their experiences in real-world "offline" settings. Comments such as "Women hide pain and protect abusers from being punished," "I dislike being a woman because women allow abuse to go on and on," and "It's hard to be women" are drawn, for instance, from what I assume was the commenters' "outside."

There was also consensus, such as the fact that women in general must be more empowered to deal with violence and abuse, although there was no agreement as to how this could be done, nor how much intervention was enough. There was general awareness that women undergoing abuse needed to be physically taken out of dangerous situations. The *etvScandal* Facebook page thus functioned as a digital "public sphere" for personal, gendered, and feminist-lite ideas and opinions about intimate partner violence, as well as sharp disagreement and polarisation. If, as Foucault (1979, p. 101) suggests, discourse is power, then the social media space provided for the collective articulation of opinions that could not have been shared in the same way before the age of social television.

Another lesson is that digital media feminist activism is influenced by language, and it became evident how Black women react to GBV in their own Indigenous ways. For instance, laughter was signposted by a neologism such as *kkkk*, and disgust by *nxa*. The use of the expression *nxa* was particularly illustrative. This expression, used to express deep disgust, is used by many Africans in sub-Saharan Africa. Verbally, it is made by sucking in air through the lips and clicking the tongue to produce a "nxa" sound. The term *nxa* itself does not exist formally in the lexicon, but is a social media invention of onomatopoeia. I observed that *nxa* was used several times to show disgust, often directed at Obakeng, but sometimes at Gloria herself. Another social media neologism used extensively was *kkkk*, to indicate humour. Such inventions subtly displaced Facebook's five pre-defined emotions, "Love," "Haha," "Wow," "Sad," or "Angry." The use of *nxa* and *kkkk* suggests an attempt to capture real-world verbal expressions in chat form, just like emojis and emoticons try to capture emotions via images typed on a keypad. Social media "talk," in this way, incorporates a creative dissidence that negotiates the proprietary Terms of Service of the respective social media platforms. Replacing Facebook's "Haha" with their own *kkkk* and Facebook's "Angry" with their own *nxa* fits this aspect of creative dissidence. Observing the humour that was going on during the "talk" and testing it against the feminist theory helped in viewing GBV with a different lens. Again, this emphasises that there is value in the comments. It is this value that this book mined for.

Humour, satire, and memes interlaced the comment threads on the etvScandal Facebook page – for example, memes of invitations to join other members in posting comments, simply saying, "if you are here for comments, please join me" and "I just came here to read comments," and displaying on the left a free sitting place on a bench and a freeze frame from *Thriller* of a young Michael Jackson eating popcorn in a cinema. There is in this meme an acknowledgement that comment threads for groups are a form of entertainment. Jokes are a social critique. For example, by being laughed at, institutions such as patriarchy lose their perceived power. Segal and Demos (2019) "talks" about agency-affirming places which women use to "talk" back" or express anger about injustices they experience. Humour can be used to represent Black women's experiences and issues that affect them, in this case GBV. Humour is an effective way to critique entrenched values about identity politics and social power inequalities, as we see in how GBV manifests itself. In addition, people used the platform to vent or laugh, to express pleasure or disgust, and so on. Hence both Obakeng and Gloria were laughed at. The audience, for instance, mocked and ridiculed Obakeng's behaviour – such as when he would call Gloria "Sunflower" despite abusing her – using this "word." However, language can quickly escalate into misogynistic comments, as the next section shows.

Misogyny or blind male machismo and masculine virility?

There were a few comments which condoned Gloria's beating and suggested solutions which were misogynistic. For instance, one suggested that instead of beating a wife, a husband could refuse to eat her food, "to teach her a lesson." Another commenter was all for revenge, stating that if Obakeng was her husband and he hit her, "he better not eat my food" because she would poison him. The debate at times would become personal, as some participants reprimanded and accused each other of being abusers and encouraging the likes of Obakeng to oppress women, or of being soft cry-babies and snowflakes who could not handle the rigours of marriage. Vitriolic attacks took the direction of "how can you, as a woman" say that? Others stated "this, coming from you a woman, is sickening," "sad to read a comment like yours, especially coming from a woman," "stupid comment from a female," "I didn't realise that you are a woman, it makes it worse," "what kind of an animal are you, you are not human," and "you are mad, if it was your mother how would you feel?", "it's men like you that make women defer marriage," and "its women like you that allow men to turn women into punching bags."

One commenter only stated that she was a woman after she received what appeared like a compliment which said, "You are the man ... you make a lot of sense." She had indicated that women were making divorce so cheap by wanting to run away from their marriages the moment they were beaten or running to the police "when husbands do silly mistakes or beat you." Although pointing out it was wrong for men to beat their wives, the commenter further argued that there were no equal rights in the marriage. As controversial as the two "women's" views were, they had every right to voice their opinions as much as those with opposing views. The bodiless space that technologies provide shielded women who would not otherwise speak their minds in public. It also made it possible for women to disguise themselves while putting their views across as best they could. Finally, it is an indication that women are not one homogenous group. No singular feminist framework can suffice to describe all women everywhere.

The contestations, as far as I could tell, broadly settled into two groups that constitute many types of feminisms discussed in this book, including Black and postmodern feminism and cyberfeminism. In postmodern feminism, people do not necessarily share the same views, even though they may all be opposing GBV. For example, some posts framed Gloria as a properly defiant, non-conformist person and an assertive independent woman who could *never* quite settle down in any marriage, but this group did not condone GBV. This view about Gloria tended to be found in the posts of those commenters who were disappointed that "the Gloria they knew" would not have stood for Obakeng's nonsense. This group tended to blame the producers of *Scandal!* for stereotyping and watering down Gloria's character to score educational points about gender violence. The other grouping included posts that, without condoning his behaviour, sympathised with Obakeng and criticised Gloria for her real or perceived flaws. The first group seemed to accord roughly with the "new school," postmodern feminists (perhaps Millennials, also known as Generation Y or the Net Generation), which I suspected would have little time for conservative notions about the real or perceived role of women. The second group appeared to consist of participants holding conservative views, the so-called "old school." The first group saw no problem, for instance, with Gloria making some money from the tripe nights and no reason why she should consult Obakeng about her every move. Being a postmodern feminist does not make one an anti-Black feminist, it simply means you are not tied to cultural beliefs and customs that violate women's rights. The second group, who might also be Black feminists, judged Gloria harshly for acting without her husband's consent. Culturally, in the African environment, the man is considered the head and the sole decision maker, and a married woman is expected to seek consent from her husband, as we discussed in Chapter 3. Gloria seemed to have good intentions for her actions, although she was not aware that she was offending her husband. The first group thus sympathised with the idea of financial independence, and the fact that a woman is autonomous from her husband. The second group blamed the "new ideas" about equality for causing strife in marriages. For this group, women must submit to their husbands. When women submit, there will be peace in the home. Suffice to say that such a debate can only end when the two sides agree to disagree.

The element of a generational clash (of ideas) persisted in many of the exchanges concerning the place of women in society, and on the question of the public/private dichotomy. A few commenters, particularly those who tended to favour limits to gender equality, admitted to being "old school." *Scandal!* is predominantly watched by middle-income women mainly in the over-15 age group, with the 25–50 age group comprising the majority of viewers (Mahlaba, 2023). When one considers that social media is a very young medium, both in terms of its age and the age of most of its users, then it is plausible that social media "talk" mostly carries the views of Millennials, or at least a generational clash of views. However, Millennials, born after the 1990s, are powerfully impacted by popular culture such as music, film, and television – particularly if they are based in urban areas where the digital divide has closed in the last decade. Their world is fast-paced, individualistic, trendy, and more postmodern than modern. It would follow that Millennials may prefer feminism in a postmodern key, since it allows for the opening of a new set of possibilities for the representation of women, work, and family, in public and in private, in "real life" and on television. It creates space for new and cross-pollinated narratives to sprout and offers creative possibilities for women. The caveat for this book is that there was no way to tell the ages of the participants in the threads.

The public/private dichotomy which sees women confined to the home, where they are seen but not heard, and where, when it concerns their bodies, they are confined to domestic spaces, has been identified by some feminists as lying at the root of patriarchal insubordination of women (cf. Das Gupta, 2007). We see Gloria facing pretty much the same predicament. Obakeng shames her, for instance, for not carrying out household chores and doing her "wifely duties" such as cooking for him. This is not only a form of stereotyping of the woman as a stay-at-home spouse, it is also an attempt to inscribe her body as good only for domestication and for gratification of male needs. Gloria, however, has desires that exceed the space of the kitchen. This leads to conflict between husband and wife. Meanwhile, Obakeng does not see any contradiction in his travelling on work assignments and enjoying the freedom that comes with such travel. It is as if men are naturally made for public spaces and the broader public realm.

The public realm is characterised by activities such as paid work and travel. In a broader framework, it includes enjoying the rights of full citizenship and exercising political and democratic rights. The private space to which Gloria is relegated, on the other hand, consists of anything that the man demarcates as the woman's natural space. This includes childbearing, satisfying male conjugal needs, motherhood, and domestic labour. Here the feminine is perceived as private and removed from politics (cf. Pateman, 1989, p. 3). This dichotomy has been met by the storm of feminist politics and activism. Of course, there are many surface changes to the traditional public/private dichotomy. For instance, many women like Gloria also engage in paid work. The dichotomy no longer strictly confines women to the home or in the kitchen. Still, as Walby (1990, p. 201) observes, exploitation of women in both the public and private arenas persists. Even where women engage in paid work, they still face segregation through pay structures that favour men. Sexual harassment is also rife, even where it is not seen, as exemplified by the recent #MeToo movement. That is, ironically, although women "are no longer restricted to the domestic hearth," they now "have the whole society in which to roam and be exploited."

During Apartheid in South Africa, women did not exist legally as full citizens, but only as minors tied to their husbands. In this context, a further example of a "whole society in which to roam and be exploited" would be a marriage contract where, although women are now subject to laws that give them definitive legal existence independent of their husbands, the wedding custom of the bride being "given away" by their father to her husband may be interpreted by men like Obakeng as justifying the subordination of women. As Pateman (1989) reminds us, although the marriage contract appears as if it is an agreement between two consenting parties of equal standing, in reality it is still predicated on a power relation of domination and subordination. Moreover, the marriage contract can be construed as giving Obakeng rights of access to Gloria's body and labour as a stay-at-home spouse. We see Gloria attempting to negotiate these constraints in various ways. She owns a house, and by holding tripe nights, she raises additional income. She also employs a helper to assist with her household chores. In this way, Gloria refuses to subsist as a strictly duty-bound wife. It is, of course, this very attempt to be nominally emancipated that creates problems between her and Obakeng.

A further example of how the oppression of women metamorphoses and moves with the times pertains to the marriage contract and property rights. Thanks to feminist activism which has turned digital where women are becoming aware of marriage, property, and inheritance rights. Black feminism, like any other feminism, is contextual. Black women are refusing to be trapped in a tradition where only men had rights in marriage, property acquisition, land rights, and inheritance. The relationship between gender-based violence and property rights for women stirred up a hornet's nest of debate. If a woman is entitled to her husband's property on divorce or death of the husband, should Obakeng not also be entitled to Gloria's property upon their divorce? Although it was wrong that, when Gloria refused to cede her rights, he beat her, was it wrong for him to claim the house as his? What does marriage mean in relation to property? In May 2022, South Africa abolished a section of the divorce law that barred those married out of community of property and without the accrual system from benefitting on divorce. This section of the law was disadvantaging many women who walked out of their marriages with nothing even though they would have contributed. This left many women trapped in abusive marriages. It remains to be seen how the change in the law will affect women in South Africa. This is a sign that postmodern views help Black feminism to move with the times.

As Head (2017) has asserted, prioritising violence against women – even to the point of seeing it as important as, for instance, getting the economy back on track – is what can radically change the situation on the ground in South Africa. The question that divides opinion, however, is still about how *exactly* to go about it in a way that is broad-based and efficacious. The success, as well as the limits, of a campaign such as #MeToo is particularly instructive in this regard, for three reasons. Firstly, it draws attention to the fact that although laws and policies enacted in the mainstream public and political realm theoretically have a sharp bearing on what happens in the private sphere, action does not march in step with legislation or formal recognition and pronouncements. The United Nations Decade for

Women, 1976–1985, has come and gone. In the 1990s, the Southern African Development Community made violence against women a regional priority. However, there is still a huge gap when it comes to how abuse is revealed and exposed. Courts of law are useless if one does not bring a case to a magistrate or judge. This is where social media and digital media feminist activism come in.

Black feminism is adaptive, while cyberfeminism shows us that the cause of women is being highlighted on social media more and more. #MeToo is a signal case, as it was driven purely by social media "talk." The movement has shown that social media "talk" can be an effective tool both for sharing personal narratives and for advocacy in tackling persistent, hidden problems women face. #MeToo is a postmodern feminist movement where previously hidden cases of sexual harassment have come to the fore, and women are using social media to refuse to be shut out as before. And, in the same way that #MeToo foregrounded sexual harassment, with victims pointing out how the campaign had made them realise how many times they had actually been sexually harassed throughout their lives without noticing it, the discussion about Gloria and Obakeng on the etvScandal Facebook page became a mirror for those facing the same abuse or those who did not realise that certain taken-for-granted norms and relations in their lives were abusive. It is perhaps no surprise that Gloria's perceived "blindness" and passivity in the face of abuse attracted the most attention. The *Scandal!* episodes, and "talk" about them on social media, thus served as consciousness-raising tools.

If, as hooks (1990) would say, there is a tendency to forget, ignore, and dismiss the existence of Black women, social media "talk" which is a postmodern feminist tool brings back some of that awareness. Instead of merely complaining and staying angry and disappointed at the lack of stories about Black women, Black women are starting to tell these stories and talking about these issues. The findings in this book suggest that social media is one way of telling these stories and talking about critical issues. Of course, such social media "talk" will need to be more grounded in the African worldview, as this book is, instead of interpreting local realities through borrowed lenses. An important example of repurposed social media "talk" is the #BlackTwitter hashtag. #BlackTwitter is not just social media, but a cultural identity built around Twitter users who focus intensely on issues of interest to the Black community. As with Black Twitter, there was no homogeneity in the ideas expressed by participants on the etvScandal Facebook page. The "talk," as it meandered, provided a dynamic opportunity for sharing narratives, points of view, and experiences as a community brought together by participants' love for a local soap opera. As Oyewumi (2005) has argued, there is a crucial need to incorporate African idioms and experiences from our social world into how we deal with gender issues, as we saw from how audiences used language to ridicule GBV in their own Indigenous language expressions. These help to make sense of our own world, in a grounded way, on our own terms.

Finally, as some commenters tended to point out, despite a consensus about how abhorrent violence against women and children is, the ever-present reality *on the ground* is that these things keep happening. Statistics show little or no reduction in the incidence and prevalence of violence. Statistics South Africa's *Victims of Crime Survey 2016/17* found that 68 per cent of South African men (nearly 10 million) did not think women deserved the same constitutional rights as men. Other surveys showed that nearly 8 per cent (12 out of a 100) of men thought it acceptable to hit a female partner during an argument. Hence, as much as the awareness on violence against women seems to be prevalent, at least in the social media chat under review there are still the 12 Obakengs out of 100 South African men who will beat up women during an argument. Digital media feminist activism exists to change that.

The very encouraging and enlightened comments on domestic violence on the etvScandal Facebook page raise the obvious question: if people are so "woke" and enlightened about domestic violence, why is South Africa still in the persistent grip of alarming statistics? Should we conclude that audiences do not actually exist in the real world? Are audiences just paying lip service to domestic violence? Could this disjunction be why some analysts define audiences as "fiction" because they sometimes do not match what they say or what they say has little relation to the real world?

The question of "inside" and "outside" raised in Chapter 4 looms large. It is still a monumental question that is hard to settle. These other questions raised here provoke many other questions in turn. Could it be that the importance attached to the role of platforms such as Facebook is exaggerated? What is the role of the various feminisms and who is really accessing social media platforms? Who is talking on them, and why? Do these viewer chats amount to anything? Do they amount to anything when one in three women is killed every day in South Africa? What are we missing? Bingwa (2018), commenting after a South African woman, Nompumelelo Mthembu, was doused with petrol, had a tyre placed around her neck, and then set alight by the estranged father of her three children, asks why it is that when women are killed by their husbands, it is not "breaking news." He asks: "Is the law listening? Is the legal system? The courts, government, parliament? Are we?"

Scandal! holds the view that GBV is a broad topic, and the Gloria/Obakeng storyline only touched on one of many angles of the problem. Since this was the television producer's first storyline on GBV, it remains to be seen what comes next. *Scandal!*'s head writer is of the opinion that before we get to what happens between Gloria and Obakeng and what we see with the GBV in general in southern Africa, there are other aspects that need to be examined. *Scandal!* argues there are many sides to blame and there is need for women to acknowledge their role and contribution, particularly to IPV. For example, what was the role of Portia (the woman who displaced Gloria in her marriage) and Obakeng's mum (who did not want her son to marry Gloria) in Gloria's abuse? The love of a mother can be disempowering to a son. This mother was an enabler. Without enablers, it is not easy to abuse women: "The fact that the son is abusive, should have been enough for a woman to say enough is enough" (Mahlaba, 2023). *Scandal!* contends that until society interrogates the perpetuation of violence by all sides, it is difficult to bring about behavioural, attitude, and mindset changes in people. Inasmuch as society may resolve GBV by arresting men, as happened to Obakeng, it may appear as if justice has been served. But until society addresses the emotional abuse caused by other women, there is a long way to go to resolve IPV. "Society needs to take a mirror and look at itself," observes Mahlaba (2023). It appears as if it is the norm for many Black women that for them to find a man, they need to fight another woman because there is a perception that there is a shortage of men.

Another angle to GBV is the unequal ground that has been created, along with reverse discrimination where society is empowering girls and women without doing the same for boys and men. This creates a situation where there are powerful women who are no longer a match for boys and men who are being left behind and have become "bitter" and feel "worthless."

Power of social media feminist activism

The producers and marketing team of *Scandal!* knowingly or unknowingly applied feminist strategies in their behavioural change approach. They used the Facebook platform primarily to drop excerpts, teasers, and trailers deliberately and strategically to cause suspense and attract viewership. They also placed "Last Night on *Scandal*" teasers to provoke audiences to "talk," and to mine such feedback as shown in Figure 5.2. Feedback is crucial in improving shows in the cut-throat ratings game. The producers would draw these trailers, cliffhangers, and teasers as marketing gimmicks from what they perceived to be the most moving, funny, and noteworthy parts of the soapie's episodes, but without producing spoilers. Whereas fan Facebook pages are created by producers and marketing departments mainly to push advertising and seek public opinion about their products, audiences are eager to "talk" about their favourite shows and to put a stamp on and own whatever little communicative space opens up.<?>

It was, and will remain, difficult to delineate and define social media "talk" participants merely from their chats. Even if someone writes their post in a certain language, there is no way of telling who they are. They may be a female or male, and they may be based in Zimbabwe, South Africa, Botswana, Namibia, or any other southern African or African country, or indeed be based anywhere in the world. Statistics from 2014 suggest that internet users are on average between 20 and 50 years old, with 51 per cent of these being women (Global Media Monitoring Report, 2015). Furthermore, if it is true that soap operas have a historically important relationship with women (Brunsdon, 2000) and that soapies are "women's terrain," then it is possible that many of the commenters could have been women. Further,

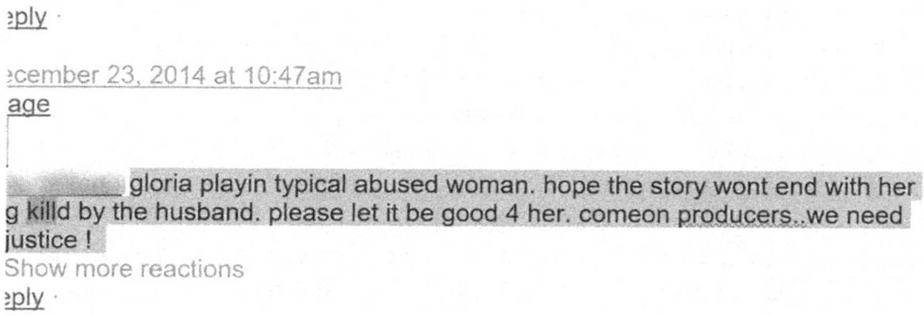

:ply ·

:cember 23, 2014 at 10:47am
age

▇▇▇▇▇ gloria playin typical abused woman. hope the story wont end with her g killd by the husband. please let it be good 4 her. comeon producers..we need justice !
Show more reactions
:ply ·

Figure 5.2 Participants did not hold back in their views

the use of a distinct internet lexicon and slang suggests that they were Millennials. But such conjecture is ultimately pointless and dangerous in our assessments of social media "talk." After all, there was enough in the comments that could be taken to be revealing that some of the commenters might have been men, since ratings data show that men follow *Scandal!* just as much as women, whether or not such men are sympathetic to women being abused. At any rate, the importance of the social media "talk" does not lie in ascriptions of gender, but rather in interpreting the value of *ways of talking*. Because the Gloria/Obakeng GBV story happened during the 16 Days of Activism, the "talk" was mostly self-generated and organic due to the uproar caused by the many women who were being murdered at the time. The content produced by the audiences was "fresh" and a "new thing" on *Scandal!* (Mahlaba, 2023). This was because social media was just beginning to pick up and the GBV topic was considered taboo. What also made a difference was the concept of audiences.

Whereas the historical definition of audience would conjure an idea of people gathered at an event or place, with the virtual spaces that have been created due to new technologies, audiences are increasingly becoming invisible and difficult to define, as we saw in Chapter 2. Baym (2011) asks, "How can we be present yet also absent?" The audience that exists in the online space is both real and intangible. Yet these sometimes faceless audiences have an even stronger voice and are not limited by fears of being visible. Audiences are faceless because even with a profile picture and name, they may not be who they say they are. In real life, they could be the opposite of what they are portraying or purporting to be. This reminds me of a cultural idiom in my local language Shona which personifies a letter in the mail as a fearless person who can deliver any message regardless of whether it is controversial or not. While the letter is not a person, it contains messages that have been crafted by a real person. Sometimes the person who crafts the letter signs it with his/her real name, but at other times it could be anonymous. In the same vein, social media audiences can have the same effect of delivering messages as bona fide commenters or anonymously. Butsch (2008, p. 4) submits that, at any rate, audience is a "situated role" and a "temporary performance."

From a feminist perspective, the invisibility of audiences has propelled digital media activism and voices that speak against topical issues such as GBV. Black women's voices that were not heard before use the anonymity of digital media to talk about matters that affect them. From a cyberfeminist view, Vasilescu et al. (2012) remind us that online users often choose gender-neutral names or opposite-sex names and profiles to cope in male-dominated environments. Where women are turned off by the blatant sexism of participants, they leave these communities. Gender-neutral names or "male profiles" may help females to be accepted by the mostly male participants. At any rate, the study that informs this book did not actively seek to establish participants' gender. Not only was it not possible, but it may not have been expressly desirable. Indeed, assessing opinions, views, and ideas without attaching them to any gender has its own methodological advantages. For instance, it allows some form of objective analysis and helps with interpretive sense-making unburdened by gender bias. What also makes the whole analysis of social media "talk" complex is that we can never really know what is going on in everyone's head when they consume and react to media texts. We thus deal with what we see on the page. What you see is what you get.

Furthermore, what was peculiar about the audience that informed this book was that it was hard to fix in place as the conversations were not among the same sets of commenters, judging from the variability in the names. Only a few names kept on reappearing, while more new people continued to join in the "talk." This fluidity of the audience thus makes it difficult to assign a definition to it. At the same time, it is hard to call them fans or a community because they do not stay in the same place long enough to constitute fandom. At the same time, social television commentators see a connection between television viewers and fandoms. This may be true considering that the main etvScandal Facebook page was established in 2005 at a time when Facebook had just launched. Fandom, indeed, is the reason behind soap opera industry professionals striving to create, as noted earlier, "a moral text that will educate and enlighten as it entertains the audiences" (Blumenthal1997, p. 111). Jenkins (2005, p. 284) describes fandom as activists "speak back," and are "assertive" and "opinionated" about their favourite programmes. Both *Scandal!* and #AmINext were not about entertainment, but dealing with a topic that daily affects families in South Africa. While television soap operas are famous because of loyalty from fans, in this case it was a unique kind of fandom which involved the discussion of a controversial topic. This kind of loyalism also opened an opportunity for the fans who were "assertive" and "opinionated," as Jenkins 2005 labels them, to share their views to help change attitudes that promote GBV.

Whereas it is hard to draw a conclusion that the same audience who watched *Scandal!* posted comments on the etvScandal Facebook page, those who proceeded to post the comments can be viewed as fans. They went beyond just watching the soap opera. That is, they appeared to have more passion, commitment, and fanaticism that drove them to and from the show to the Facebook page. At any rate, as Busse and Gray (2011) suggest, there is no longer one type of fan. Old, normative definitions no longer hold. There is now much fluidity and variability involved. Furthermore, if one accepts Jenkins's assertions (2005), then these are fans because they are part of a (feminine?) discourse which others may conceive as "gossip," but which helps to "transform issues of public concern into topics of personal significance." Baym (2000) refers to earlier forums as having been like a "base" on which "strong traditions and a clear identity group" were built. She viewed a given forum as a "social world that felt like a community" because the audience stayed on the forum over time. The Facebook fans of *Scandal!*, on the other hand, were elusive and always changing.

Although this variability made for an eclectic mix of opinions and broadened the realm of the conversation, the reason for the ever-shifting audience is a subject that needs further investigation in future studies. Still, all the participants seemed familiar with the television soapie. At least, none indicated otherwise. From this point of view at least, the audience may be viewed as a genuine community. In the past, the private and intimate discourse of gossip provided an opportunity for women to discuss controversial concerns in a forum considered free of patriarchal influence because gossip was "frivolous and silly," and hence was only associated with women. Social media such as Facebook appear to provide new alternative forums for discussing these topical issues.

Despite the ever-evolving nature of the audience, it was noted that the "talk" somehow continued uninterrupted. This can be partly attributed to technology which allows such conversations to continue if one has access to the internet and to Facebook, and a sustained interest in the topic to want to add their opinion or "like" what is being said. Facebook becomes the meeting point of minds and interests, albeit ephemerally. Part of this convergence is captured in what Facebook's Mark Zuckerberg once said when he, talking about Facebook, stated that "we exist at the intersection of technology and social issues" (Lee, 2011, p. xiii). The ceaseless flow of commenters meant that those who join in at this point or that get to comment on posts by those who have already left the conversation, and so on and so forth. This is what sets apart digital media feminist activism from other of feminist channels because it offers a platform that enables conversation to be ongoing. The platform is open to anyone who wishes to contribute their voice if they have access to the internet and are connected to social media. This type of digital media audience is different from before Facebook was introduced because in the past, people would have to converge at some physical place to have this "thread" of conversation. This is important for digital media feminist activism because, as stated earlier, these kinds of "talk" where multitudes of people can chat concurrently regardless of geographical location and time were well nigh impossible in the pre-social media era, hence it was difficult to spread feminist ideas. The convergence of two media platforms, television and social media, resulted in a multi-communication flow of ideas, in that audiences had a chance to react to what they were watching on television through Facebook in real time. Aaker, Smith, and Adler (2010) state that matching distinct media types with distinct audiences allows for more engagement and empowerment. In the same way that, before the invention of printing and writing, sender and receiver needed to be in the same space and time for communication to occur, the pre-social media era in the 20th century and early 21st century offered no way of tapping into the worlds of viewing audiences in real time. This made it harder to combat GBV, but all this has changed drastically in the last decade.

Digital media activism is a highly unique way of interacting as it often leaves traces of audiences' consumption practices, as they comment on texts. Documenting these, as this book does, is a feminist act, and is important in building a new media feminist trajectory. There is an acknowledgement that books such as this one that are based on research on digital media activism take a closer look at audiences' interaction online and help add new knowledge about audience participation online, as (Couldry, 2011) observed.

Whatever uses the social media platform was put to, the audiences became, as Graham and Hajru (2011, p. 18) observed, *deliberating publics* using the talking points provided by the producers (or by other commenters) and the communicative spaces offered by social media pages, features, and tools. Those against forms of women's oppression such as GBV use these talking points to spread their ideas and to be heard. This sort of activism helps to set the agenda on the broader feminist politics of which GBV is a big part. As noted earlier, the agenda-setting on gender violence did not begin with the "Last Night on *Scandal*" teasers and trailers. Rather, it began much, much earlier, with the script and the producers of the show. Judging from the posts studied, the agenda of *Scandal!* seemed to be not only to raise awareness about gender-based violence, but to initiate debate around the topic in a bid to generate dialogue as well as help foster behavioural change among audiences to counter domestic violence, including changing mindsets of audiences on how to deal with conflict in relationships. What this book did was to subject the ideas from the digital audiences to feminist scrutiny. A feminist framing of digital media activism on key topics such as GBV helps to change both attitudes and behaviour and to tackle the root causes. Using different theoretical frameworks from the one used in this book might not have centralised the GBV issue in the context of how women are affected and may have missed the knowledge of GBV and how it affects ordinary Black women, something that is critical to behavioural change.

Scholars such as Levine (1985) had seen social media coming, but without knowing what it was going to look like or how it was going to change the media landscape and impact feminism. Levine, at the time, commented presciently on the need for television soap opera producers to find innovative ways of communicating with their fans. Levine noted that there were opportunities for shows not only to learn from viewers, but to develop direct ways of communicating "with them, potentially providing soapies with avenues for testing ideas with viewers ahead of time and fostering feelings of collaboration amongst soap opera fans and the industry." Levine even speculated about the "significant advertising and other revenue opportunities" that would come with that. In the 1990s, she observed that fans were using the internet to communicate about their shows. Her prediction may have exceeded expectations because of the opportunities created for fans to "talk" back and for activists to use such platforms as tools to create their own cultural identities. This, of course, does not downplay the downside of such platforms being used as tools for misogyny and oppression.

Levine reckoned that soap opera producers would use these comments to improve their productions and take into consideration viewers' suggestions and feedback to keep their ratings high. It was also at this time that internet soap opera bulletin board messages and chatrooms mushroomed. A notable aspect of these phenomena was their ability to offer marginalised groups such as women space to discuss issues of concern publicly. However, these spaces never grew in stature, accessibility, and ease of use in the way Facebook, which boasts of a billion daily users, eventually did. Up until the creation of social media, it was virtually impossible to have simultaneous multi-media interaction regardless of geographical space and time. The usual main limitation to this type of "talk" was the interface. Using online spaces has, however, altered how people interact and engage. The easy linkability of online material helps spread messages faster and wider, at times trending and going viral, which is what currently helps the digital media activism that has given birth to the online feminist cultural groups that are widely known such as #MeToo, #AmINext and #BlackLivesMatter.

The feminist analysis in this book goes as far as observing the acting style of a character, or their perceived character strengths or flaws. From a feminist perspective, observing this representation was important. For example, at times, participants would react to the storyline of a particular episode. The Facebook page would thus be used as a communication platform for the audience to express their views and opinions, perceptions, attitudes, and knowledge about the characters in the soap opera, providing a running commentary on the quality of the work of the producers, directors, and scriptwriters, and reflecting on how the participants' everyday lives measured up to the soapie, and vice versa. The representation of Gloria and how she responded to GBV were critiqued. Digital media feminist activism is helping to redefine cultural identity for women. The nature and content of the "talk" allowed the platform to play a central role in the construction and contestation of meanings about intimate partner violence, and revealed intimate details drawn from the participants' own offline lives. The unspoken became spoken, and the invisible visible.

The analysis for this book also examined the nature of the "talk" itself in terms of style and "expression." For instance, some commented at length, while some did so only in monosyllables. Some just "Liked" the page or "Loved" it, while others responded through a variety of emojis. The way this "talk" is written is immensely creative, but is good for activism as people speak in an informal way. However, it poses spelling and syntactic challenges because postings are rarely in full sentences or observe formal spelling and grammar. There is no due attention to normative writing rules. There are no Facebook rules against inventing one's own "language," grammar, spelling, and syntax. Hence words are often shortened and invented. For instance, "is" may be written "z," "why" as "y," "people" as "Ppl," "greatest of all time" as "GOAT," "great" as "gr8," "family" as "fam," "to be honest" as "tbh," "in my opinion" as "imo," "lit" means "awesome," and so on. In such a lexicon, "salty" means a bitter person, "sus" means scandalous, "extra" means one is trying too hard, "clapback" is to respond cleverly to negativity, "Bible" means you are speaking the truth, and "woke" means clever. Sometimes the "talk" was a running "pitchside" commentary or umpiring directed at the characters, such as "err Gloria don't defend him maan [man], he will hit you again and again, and again!", "Why do you keep defending the fool?", "Gloria is being abused *mara* [but] shes [she's] too blind to see," and so on.

This invention and use of a new lexicon indicated that the commenters could have been mostly Millennials. If formal language demonstrates professionalism, authority, and seriousness, the language of social media "talk" is informal, conversational, and unstructured and has a personality and warmth that resonates with many people. It can be emotional, serious, angry, disrespectful, or funny. But it is never dry or lacking in warmth or personality. It is these qualities that identify such discourse as "talk" because it is very close to how we would "talk" in real-world settings. This kind of "talk" is ideal for activism because it is classless. Whether someone is elite, middle-class, ordinary, or poor, if they have access to social media platforms, they can easily join in the conversations and find it easier to express themselves. People seldom use formal language and punctuation in everyday conversations, as this would be very weird. Such slang can also be rich in meaning. As G. K. Chesterton said, "All slang is metaphor, and all metaphor is poetry." The lexicon of social media "talk," apart from being whimsical (or perhaps because it is whimsical) also has a short life span, and some of the words that were popular and in use in 2014 are no longer in use now. A few, however, have endured.

Still on the subject of language, social media "talk" of the kind found in South Africa is intensely multilingual. That is, English is not the only medium of communication used. Rather, participants used their own Indigenous languages such as Sotho, Tswana, Zulu, Shona, Xhosa, Ndebele, and Afrikaans, among others, to express themselves. It was not uncommon to see three languages – English, Shona, and Zulu – in one sentence. Although there is a translation button, some of the translations hardly makes sense, more so because the words may not be not spelt out in full. The use of local idioms and slang on top of the usual internet lexicon makes social media "talk" a completely new beast in terms of expression, as we will examine later. One not only has to know what the English slang words mean, but uniquely South Africa lingo such as *mara*, *bathong*, and *haaibo!*" Facebook is transformed into a marketplace of ideas and knowledge as well as language, metaphor, and idioms. As Baym (2000) succinctly argues, this type of "talk" is different from the verbal "talk" we know because there is no body movement, vocal tone, rate, or volume. This is perfect for digital media activism such as feminism.

This "talk" is also different in another sense: if the audiences were put in a room to engage in this type of conversation, there would be Babel, chaos, and unbearable noise. Social media "talk" cannot exist anywhere else but on social media. There is much "conversational chaos," creativity, creative destruction, and invention that is uniquely involved. The audiences would be talking to each other, but at the same time "talk" past each other. This is not good for activism, as meaning may be lost. At times, someone would say what they were thinking, not necessarily replying to the other. One posting would be addressed to the administrators, while the next comment would pose questions to the characters. Yet another post would be responding to what others had commented on or addressing other fans. It was hard to create consistently coherent threads of the conversation. Without the kind of analysis the data was subjected to, it would not have been possible to take meaning from the comments, let alone the feminist interpretation of the posts. It can be concluded that social media is creating conversation norms that are different from what we know and understand. Audiences get to pick conversations they want to react or respond to at the time they want to. At the same time, this variability and "conversational chaos" do not stop the conversations. The process of sense-making is thus challenging for any researcher, but at the same time not impossible. What it does is disrupt the normative process of interpersonal and mass communication while setting up its own forms of "talk." When people gather in an online space to "talk" about a television show, they become a mass audience, yet the messages directed to individuals within the group are interpersonal while also being mass communication because they are available for all to read (Baym, 2011). So what is personal becomes mass, causing private spaces to increasingly connect and overlap with public spaces (Morley, 2010; Blossom, 2009, p. 31), which is what makes digital media activism impactful. Still, there is reward in the fact that participants consistently experience their online interaction as "talk."

Social media "talk" and freedom of expression

Whereas soap operas traditionally have been associated with commodity fetishism, consumerism, domesticity, and smut – seen in recycled plotlines of extramarital affairs and other issues relating to cheating and deceiving – the episodes examined here focus on intimate partner violence – a hidden problem because it occurs in the confines of people's homes and other private spaces. The assumed "safe spaces" are, more and more, a "cradle of violence." Showing topical issues such as intimate partner violence on television, and sustained interest and discussion on platforms such as Facebook, are integral to the long-term goal of tackling such problems by and from the roots.

Soaps are so compelling to their audiences that they make them believe they are getting to know about people and life. Gloria and Obakeng were thus viewed by social media audiences as "real." Ilse van Hemert, the producer of *Scandal!*, even stated to *TVPlus* magazine that she hoped that audiences would be able to separate Peter Moruakgomo from Obakeng. She said, "we discussed that some people may even confuse Obakeng with Peter and attack him personally for what his character is doing to Gloria, especially since Peter is such a convincing actor. So, guys don't slap Peter please!"[2] The use of veiled threats by some in the audience, such as "I want to meet with [Obakeng] for advice" or castrate Obakeng and "feed it to the dogs so that he learns to respect women," do indicate that there is some justification for Hemert's concerns about possible danger to Moruakgomo. Such threats also show the thin line between "inside" and "outside," online and offline discussed in Chapter 4. One participant even posted a comment suggesting that if no one was going to do it, they were going to rescue Gloria themselves. Sunden (2002) postulates that when people "talk" about a television programme, they inevitably "talk" about themselves as well. I observed that this seemed to be the case in roughly 20 per cent of comments, thus revealing, on the one hand, what I assumed were ever-present and ongoing concerns about gender violence in their everyday lives and, on the other hand, a persistent merging of fiction and reality and of "outside" and "inside." What audiences raised on *Scandal!* was not different from what people posted during the #AmINext campaign against real murders of women in South Africa.

The convergence of the "outside" and "inside" coupled with online anonymity provided a space where there was willingness to "talk," share, express opinions, vent feelings, disagree, and troll about gender-based violence. There was, for instance, intermittent discussion of the meaning of women's emancipation and whether freedom and equality were possible in all spaces, such as private and public, home and work. Equality is defined as sameness in terms of social status or legal and or political rights, although there is a whole debate globally about what the term "equality" means (Pilcher and Whelehan, 2004, p. 37). Some participants did not believe that independence, freedom, and equality for women could be enjoyed equally in all spaces. Rather, there were times when it applied only at work and not at home, or in public and not in private, and so on. That is, women's independence and equality were an ongoing negotiation. Context, for some, mattered more in the negotiation. The idea that customarily in African homes the man is the presumed head of the house still obtains in various diffracted forms. This was so even in cases where Obakeng's capability to provide for his family was impaired or where Obakeng did not even own the house he claimed to be head of.

Even more interestingly, the family or home were considered by some commenters to be a private space which was closed to interference by outsiders and strangers. Of course, this privacy and "domesticity" is also why domestic violence is by and large hard to detect. Also, this non-interference in the "privacy" of the home can lead to a legitimisation of male power in cases such as domestic violence. It appeared from the comments that how some women in African contexts react in the family has a lot to do with their own *socialisation* and how they were brought up. Socialisation, in as far as it is a process of acquiring what one knows, informs one's cultural standpoint, knowledge, and belief systems, acquired through the society one lives in, the language, formal or informal rules of behaviour, and sets of knowledge. It was clear that the participants in the discussion were not homogenous. For instance, some commenters believed that the emancipation of women has (and needs) limits, while others regarded it as an appropriate ideal that, one day, can be reached. One participant who used a masculine name in her chats described herself as a married woman from the "old school" who regarded the man as the uncontested head of the house. She blamed "so-called equality" for destroying the "fabric" of marriage. In her view, women nowadays lack toughness, divorce easily, and allege abuse unnecessarily. This commenter thought Gloria was impolite and not exemplary enough for her children. For instance, she accused Gloria of lying and doing as she pleased without consulting her husband as she should have done, and of being excessively materialistic. Of course, she put out the disclaimer that her views should not be taken to mean that she supported abuse.

It is instructive that this "old school" participant's views on marriage were not shared by most participants, which is why feminism can never be one thing. The other participants, while agreeing that Gloria might be imperfect, argued that the issue of violence must be viewed and treated separately and must *never* be condoned. There was thus active disagreement and lack of consensus on the central issues. One commenter asked, incredulously, "How could one condone abuse?" and "Would you want that for your kid?" These disagreements were not a bad thing. Rather, social media "talk" is predicated on what Bailey (2005, p. 70) calls "drawing different types of knowledge." The "talk" necessarily brought out varied and differentiated views. This could be put down, among other things, to differences in the participants' experiences, and their worldviews and ways of making meaning. As noted, the commenter who appeared to justify Obakeng's actions clearly stated that she was not condoning women abuse, although she was still labelled as doing so.

Indeed, some audiences took the "reality show" to extremes as they went as far as giving unsolicited advice, solutions, and reconstructed scenarios to the producers of *Scandal!* about how they thought Gloria should have handled her situation. For instance, one commenter said: "abusive hypocrites don't change so Gloria don't forgive him," another chipped in, saying, "why are you defending this dog?" As we will see, there was a visceral response from the commenters against intimate partner abuse, expressed in a widespread condemnation of Obakeng in the Facebook comments, which I can characterise as feminist – or at least feminist-lite – in nature. As pointed out in Chapter 3, feminism is a framework placed in the service of social justice. Its core function as an approach is to remind us that we can imagine a world where women are full human beings who are not made in the image of patriarchy. As Pynta et al. (2014, p. 1) point out, the rise of digital technology has seen "a fundamental shift in the way media is consumed." The participation provoked by Obakeng's abuse of Gloria is not just passive consumption of media, but some kind of consumption-with-participation. Fragmented consumption and time-shifted viewing have altered the traditional passive role. Interestingly, despite the increased participation, there is little evidence that the producers of *Scandal!* really listened to audiences and changed their storyline to placate the viewers. Rather, it seems more plausible that the storyline unfolded as intended. Still, the participants were pleased and satisfied that their "advice" had been heeded by the show's producers.

Who we are and how we relate to others is partly a matter of identity construction, and social media "talk" sheds some light on the processes of self-representation and the formation of identities in the online space. The expression of opinions, in this case, was made possible by the soap opera, which gave the fans of the soap a common interest, and by the social media platform which enabled the "talkers" to discourse in a particular way. Spence (2001) argues that soap opera characters cannot be dismissed as merely fictional – they are "true enough to be able to draw moral conclusions, forming opinions, and make comparisons from what they knew from the real world." People's self-reported experiences with domestic violence helped them connect with Gloria and Obakeng's story. This prior experience made it more likely that pieces of the audience's own experience would "infiltrate the screen" (Spence, 2001, p. 188). What, then, is the conclusion of this digital media activism in this book?

Notes

1 E-Buzz (12 January 2015) "Tshepo Mosese celebrates 10 years of Scandal!". http://www.etv.co.za/news/2015/01/12/tshepo-mosese-celebrates-10-years-scandal/. Accessed 26 September 2016.
2 https://www.pressreader.com/south-africa/tv-plus-south-africa/20141112/284073434942665.

References

Aaker, J., Smith, A., & Adler, C. 2010. *The dragon fly effect: Quick, effective and powerful ways to use social media, to driver social change*. San Francisco, CA: Jossey-Bass.

Abrahams, N., Mathews, S., Martin, L., Lombard, C., & Jewkes, R. (2013). Intimate partner femicide in South Africa in 1999 and 2009. *PLoS Medicine*, 10(4), e1001412. https://doi.org/10.1371/journal.pmed.1001412.

Adichie, C.N. (2009). The danger of a single story. Home page. https://www.ted.com/talks/chimamanda_ngozi_adichie_the_danger_of_a_single_story/c Accessed 2016/02/29.

Adichie, C.N. (2014). Chimamanda Ngozi Adichie: 'I decided to call myself a happy feminist'. Home page. https://www.theguardian.com/books/2014/oct/17/chimamanda-ngozi-adichie-extract-we-should-all-be-feminists. Accessed 2016/02/29.

Ayiera, E. (2010). Sexual violence in conflict: A problematic international discourse. *Feminist Africa Issue*, 14, 7–18.

Bailey, S. (2005). *Media audiences and identity: Self-construction in the fan experience*. New York: Palgrave Macmillan.

Baym, N.K. (2000). *Tune in, log on: Soaps, fandom and online community*. London: Sage Publications.

Baym, N.K. (2011). *Connections in the digital age*. Cambridge: Polity Press.

Blossom, J. (2009). *Content nation: Surviving and thriving as social media changes our work, our lives and our future*. Fishers, IN: Wiley Publishing.

Blumenthal, D. (1997). *Women and soap opera: A cultural feminist perspective*. London: Praeger Publishers.

Bingwa, B. (2018). Bingwa asks why is it when women are killed by their husbands it's not "breaking news". Home page. https://www.702.co.za/articles/303199/bongani-the-heavens-have-long-stopped-listening-to-women-like-nompumelelo. Accessed 2018/5/23.

Brunsdon, C. (2000). *The feminist, the housewife and the soap opera*. Oxford: Clarendon press.

Busse, K., &, Gray, J. (2011). Fan cultures and fan communities. In Nightingale, V. (Ed), *The handbook of media audiences*. Chichester: Blackwell Publishing, pp. 452–443.

Butsch, R. (2008). *The citizen audience: Crowds, publics, and individuals*. New York: Routledge.

Chambers, D. (2005). Comedies of sexual morality and female singlehood. In Lockyer, S. & Pickering, M. (Eds), *Beyond a joke: The limits of humour*. Basingstoke: Palgrave Macmillan, pp. 1–24.

Couldry, N. (2011). The necessary future of the audience…and how to research it. Nightingale, V. (Ed), *The handbook of media audiences*. Chichester: Blackwell Publishing, pp. 213–239.

Das Gupta, S. (2007). *Body evidence intimate violence against South Asian women in America*. London: Rutgers University Press.

Dobash, R.E., & Dobash, R.P. (1977). Wives: The appropriate victims of martial violence. *Victimology*, 2, 436–442.

Foucault, M. (1979). *Discipline and punish: The birth of the prison*. New York: Vintage.

Fuchs, C. (2017). *Social media. A critical introduction* (Second Edition). London: Sage.

Geraghty, C. (2001). Social issues and realist soaps: A study of British soaps in the 1980/1990s. In Allen, R.C. (Ed.), *To be continued... Soaps around the world*. London: Routledge, pp. 66–80.

Graham, T., & Hajru, A. (2011). Reality TV as a trigger of everyday political talk in the net-based public sphere. *European Journal of Communication*, 26(1), 18–32.

Global Media Monitoring Project. (2015). *Who makes the news?* London: World Association for Christian Communication. Home page. https://www.media-diversity.org/additional-files/Who_Makes_the_News_-_Global_Media_Monitoring_Project.pdf. Accessed 2018/02/21.

Head, T. (2017). How South Africa fails miserably to save women from gender violence. Home page. https://www.thesouthafrican.com/how-south-africa-still-fails-to-protect-women-from-gender-violence/. Accessed 2018/05/21.

Habermas, J. (1989b). The public sphere: An encyclopaedia article. In Bronner, S.E. & Kellner, D. (Eds), *Critical theory and society: A reader*. New York: Routledge, pp. 136–142.

hooks, b. (1990). *Yearning*. Boston, MA: South End.

Jenkins, H. (2005). "Buy these problems because they're fun to solve: A conversation with Will Wright. *Telemedium: The Journal of Media Literacy*, 52(1&2), 20–23.

Joachim, J.M. (2007). *Agenda setting, the UN, and the NGOs: Gender violence and reproductive rights*. Washington, DC: Georgetown University Press.

Kozinets, R.V. (2015). *Netnography redefined* (Second Edition). London: Sage Publications.

Lee, N. (2011). *Facebook nation: Total information awareness*. New York: Springer.

Levine, E. (1985). "What the hell does TIIC mean?" Online content and the struggle to save the soaps. In Ang, I. (Ed), Watching Dallas. *Soap opera and the melodramatic imagination*. London: Methuen, pp. 201–208.

Mahlaba, G. (2023). WhatsApp interview. Johannesburg. 14 February. Interview notes available from the author.

Mann, K.L. (2014). What can feminism learn from new media? *Communication & Critical/Cultural Studies*, 11(3), 293–297, Communication & Mass Media Complete, EBSCOhost, viewed 17 June 2017.

Morley, D. (2010). The reconfigured home. In Berry, C., Kim S., &. Spigel, L. (Eds), *Electronic Elsewhere: Media, technology, and the experience of social space*. Minneapolis, MN: University of Minnesota Press, pp. 3–15.

Oyewumi, O. (2005). Visualising the body: Western theories and African subjects. In Oyewumi, O. (Ed), *African gender studies: A reader*. Basingstoke, Great Britain: Palgrave Macmillan, pp. 3–21.

Pateman, C. (1989). *The disorder of women*. Cambridge: Polity.

Phiri, M. (2021). Coronavirus satire: A dissection of feminist politics and humour. In Mpofu, S. (Eds), *Digital humour in the Covid-19 pandemic*. Cham: Palgrave Macmillan. https://doi.org/10.1007/978-3-030-79279-4_8.

Pilcher, J., & Whelehan, I. (2004). *Fifty key concepts of gender studies*. London: Sage Publications.

Porter, D. (1977). Soap time: Thoughts on a commodity art form. College English. *Mass Culture, Political Consciousness, and English*, 38(8), 782–788.

Pynta, P., Seixas, S.A.S., Nield, G.E., Hier, J., Millward, E., & Silberstein, R.B. (2014). The power of social television: Can social media build viewer engagement? A new approach to brain imaging of viewer immersion. *Journal of Advertising Research*, 54(1), 71–80.

Reinharz, S. (1992). *Feminist methods in social research*. Oxford: Oxford University Press.

Robinson, V., & Richardson, D. (Eds). (1997). *Introducing Women's Studies* (Second Edition). Basingstoke: Macmillan.

Segal, M.T., & Demos, V. (2019). *Gender and the media: Women's places*. Bingley: Emerald Publishing Limited.

Spence, L. (2001). They killed off Marlena, but she's on another show now: Fantasy, reality, and pleasure in watching daytime soap operas. In Allen, R.C. (Ed), *To be continued ... soap operas around the world*. London: Routledge, pp. 182–198.

Sundén, J. (2002). I'm still not sure she's a she. Textual talk and typed bodies in online interaction. In McIlvenny, P. (Ed), *Talking gender and sexuality*. Amsterdam: John Benjamins Publishing, pp. 289–312.

Vasilescu, B., Capiluppi, A., & Serebrenik, A. (2012). Gender, representation, and online participation: A quantitative study of stack overflow, Social informatics 2012 International Conference on social informatics, proceedings of a conference, IEEE Computer Society, Washington DC, pp. 332–338.

Walby, S. (1990). *Theorising patriarchy*. Oxford: Blackwell.

Epilogue

Although this book is not conclusive, it is important in revealing how old and new forms of media meet to tackle one of the world's pressing problems of GBV, and critically examines the role of digital media feminist activism. Its wiewpoint has a feminist bias in examining how people view GBV among marginalised Black women. Television watching is no longer an isolated activity, due to smartphones, tablets, and computers which allow soap opera producers to facilitate a new form of social media "talk" aimed at helping to change social behaviour to deal with difficult and controversial topics such as GBV. This "talk" is helping to form new feminist cultural identities as digital media activism takes root and utilises every opportunity to confront issues that affect women on digital platforms. The culture of oppressing women is being broken down by people who are speaking out on these digital media platforms. Even without mentioning the word "feminism," feminist practices and cultures are being built as people use the new digital media platforms to reject patriarchal oppression. The GBV cases of poor or ordinary Black township women, whose voices are not often heard in the media, are now being highlighted in ways that help us understand the nature of GBV and the challenges these women face. These digital media activists are building new feminist trajectories that resonate with their own cultures where women use the power of the media to generate offline actions that help to change how they are perceived and treated. For example, the "talk" reveals a convergence of cultural ideas around marriage and GBV. Social media is thus part of an Indigenous knowledge production process where people produce homegrown solutions in their own Indigenous languages. There is a general awareness of GBV's complex nature, such as its causes, solutions, and cycles of violence. The meeting point of the online and offline, suggests that social media "talk" mirrors reality. It brings the invisible to the fore and makes the private public. Although violence against women, particularly femicide, is generally not condoned by social media audiences, the "talk" reveals that GBV among marginalised women can be exacerbated by challenges such as stereotypes, misrepresentation, under-representation of Black women in the media, and misogyny. These issues, coupled with historic challenges such as toxic masculinity, the manufacture of female fear, the manosphere, and lack of tackling the root causes, such as patriarchy and structural violence, remain among the obstacles to eliminating GBV. Future studies should lean towards how these forms of social media "talk" can be analysed further to map and create Indigenous feminist knowledge and smart solutions for GBV.

Subjecting this digital media activism to feminist analysis helped to observe that members did not merely comment on *Scandal!*, but used the platform to "speak" to *Scandal!*'s producers or broadcast their own messages to other fans. This is the activism of digital media, because it always involves action. Action that challenges any kind of oppression against women becomes feminist, whether you mention the word or not. Feminism theory helps to redefine the position of women and women's expectations. The uniqueness of this book is its attempt to focus on gender violence against Black township women such as Gloria, who are rarely portrayed in the mainstream media, but whose voices are now being amplified through social media. This digital media activism has helped to re-contextualise GBV although sadly, South Africa's inequality and structural violence result in this type of activism remaining a purview of a few elite women.

This calls, for instance, for understanding the socio-cultural nature of gender violence. Other interventions include exploring the critical role the media can play in educating audiences *against* violence against women. The seminal example is the #AmINext hashtag, where the GBV discourses are emerging and circulating on social media. The book is an attempt to explore the role social media plays both in our conception and misconception of violence against women.

A core aspect of the discourse of violence against women is not just to highlight the extent and complexity of the problem, but to tease out rigorous explanations that may lead us closer and closer to eradicating the epidemic. One aspect of the search for explanations, in my view, is to examine how society "talks" about violence against women such as we see on *Scandal!* and #AmINext. Social media "talk" relies on the relationship between language, discourse and meaning (Wodak, 1997; Fairclough, 2013, p. 7). Digital media feminism is capitalising on these three. Sayyid and Zac (1998, p. 249) remind us that reality is accessible through the descriptions made by language. Descriptions, through language, have an important influence on how we understand and interpret reality, as we witness on *Scandal!* and #AmINext – for example, in the way audiences define issues such as marriage, inheritance, and violence. Descriptions of the world are how we socially construct reality. Language is "man-made" and a carrier of ideas, whereas discourse focuses primarily on the meaning of "talk" or text (Cameron, 1990, p. 14; Mills, 2008, p. 43; Cook, 2008). Reality is constructed through naming and defining (Mills, 2008, p. 43) – a process from which women have historically been excluded. Mills (2008) regards language as a system which benefits and accords value to the experiences and beliefs of men more than those of women. Spender (1980, p. 84) argues that by altering the terms within a language which represent women negatively, one also potentially transforms the way that women are normatively thought about. It is my view that how people "talk" about an issue such as gender violence, the meanings they attach to it, and the way they represent it in language are crucial to forming a nuanced view of not only what motivates violence against women, but also how to deal with it. Currently, the best place to find people "talking" about an issue *in a certain way* (or ways) is, without doubt, high-octane word of mouth: social media (Bell, 2010, p. 11). This book therefore examined how we "talk" about violence against women using this high-octane word of mouth, and what these kinds of "talk" reveal about personal, social, cultural, and moral attitudes towards GBV.

Social media is important to digital media feminist activism because it inserts things into social discourse in a hyper-mediated way that is unlike anything we have known prior to the 2000s. Traditional discourse could never be "high-octane." At the same time, social media may get as "high-octane" as it likes, but it is still people "chatting," it is still word of mouth. As high-octane word of mouth, social media is primarily a mode of communication. Whether or not people change their behaviour requires other variables to change as well, not just communication. But how and what we communicate is an important and invaluable starting point.

References

Bell, J. (2010). *Socialise the enterprise*. The Red Papers. New York: Ogilvy & Mather.
Cook. K.E. (2008). Discourse. In Given, L.M. (Ed), *The Sage encyclopaedia of qualitative research methods*, Volumes 1 & 2. London: Sage, pp. 216–217.
Cameron, D. (1990). *The feminist critique of language: A reader* (First Edition). London: Routledge.
Fairclough, N. (2013). *Critical discourse analysis: The critical study of language* (Second Edition). New York: Routledge.
Mills, S. (2008). *Language and sexism*. Cambridge: Cambridge University Press.
Sayyid, B., & Zac, L. (1998). Political analysis in a world without foundations. In Scarbrough, E., & Tanenbaum, E. (Eds), *Research strategies in the social sciences*. Oxford: Oxford University Press, pp. 249–267.
Spender, D. (1980). *Man-made language*. London: Routledge.
Wodak, R. (1997). Introduction. In Wodak, R. (Ed), *Gender and discourse*. Sage: London, pp. 1–20.

Index

16 Days of Activism 7–8, 48
365 Days for No Violence Against Women and Children 8

Aaker, J. 105
Abrahams, Y. 66
abuse: Gloria's passive acceptance of 87–89; psychological 13; *see also* violence
activism 6, 116; fandom 35
Adesina, O. 55
Adichi, C. 87, 92
Adler, C. 105
advertising 39
Africa/n: feminism 46, 52, 54, 59–60; identity 55; matriarchal system 52–53, 55; patriarchy 51–52
"Africanness" 39
Allen, R. C. 38
Amadiume, I. 44–45, 52–53, 55, 58
#AmINext 1, 2, 6, 18, 34–35, 38, 47, 48, 56–57, 65, 77–78, 80, 82; "inside"/"outside" discourse 75–76; petitions 81; as public sphere 93–94; *see also* digital media feminist activism
Ang, I. 34–35
Angelou, M. 17
Antrobus, P. 8, 59, 60, 65–66
Apartheid 18, 39, 54, 57–58, 97–98; *see also* South Africa/n
audience/s 34–35, 102–105; soap operas 38–39
Ayiera, E. 21, 87

Bailey, S. 110–111
Baym, N. 22, 32–33, 39, 102, 104, 108
Bingwa, B. 100

Black feminism 39, 45–46, 54–60, 96–98; diversity of 59
Black sisterhood 58
Black women: stereotypes 9, 86–87; stigma 87–88
#BlackLivesMatter movement 58
#BlackTwitter 99
Blumenthal, D. 40, 47
Booysen, A. 6
#BringBackOurGirls movement 72
Britton, H. 43
Brown, R. 39
Brunsdon, C. 39, 40
Burton, N. 39
Busse, K. 104
Butsch, R. 103

Canada 80
Capiluppi, A. 49–50
Carrillo, R. 5
change.org 81
Chase, K., *The Spectacle of Intimacy* 11
Chesterton, G. K. 107
Choja, O. 49–50
Civil Rights movement 57
clicktivism 79–80; *see also* digital media feminist activism
colonialism 52, 60
common couple violence 12–13
community 30–31
#CountMeIn 8
creative dissidence 94
Crenshaw, K. 57
Crumpton, S. M. 9
cyberculture 61
cyberfeminism 46, 61–63, 77, 99

Dangarembga, T. 47
Davis, A. 45, 57
death penalty 81
deconstruction 64
Demos, V. 94–95
Denfeld, R. 65
digital media feminist activism 1, 2, 5–7, 18, 34, 43, 44, 60, 61, 64, 72, 78–79, 81–82, 86, 91–93, 104–105, 115; hashtags 75, 76; sense of community 30; social television 31; "spreadable media" 31
Diop, C. A. 60
discourse 63; *see also* "talk"
discrimination 50; reverse 101
diversity, in Black feminism 59
Dlamini, N. 6
Dobash, R. P. 91, 92
domestic violence 2, 3, 65, 90, 110; emotional trauma 17

East, J. F. 64
edutainment 7
Ellard, J. H. 15
equality 96, 109–110
ethnography 22
etvScandal Facebook page 86, 90, 100, 103; humour 94–95; as public sphere 93–94

Facebook 1, 2, 25, 71–72, 75, 104; access 93; fan pages 32; friends 32–33, 72; "Like" button 23–24, 33; *Scandal!* page 33, 34, 38–40; "What's on your mind?" 32; *see also* social media
family 38, 110; violence 22
fans and fandom 32, 35, 103–104; meta text 34; *Scandal!* 33, 34
fear 19
femicide 80; Löwstedt on 19; in South Africa 5–6, 18, 57–58
Femicide National Strategic Plan Steering Committee 1
femininity 51
feminism/feminist theory 1–3, 5–7, 23, 43, 44, 50, 111, 115; African 46, 54, 59–60; Black 39, 45–46, 54–60, 96–98; cyber 46, 61–63, 99; patriarchy 51–52; postmodern 46, 63–66, 96; representation 91; role of men in 59–60; second wave 53; South African 53, 54; Ubuntu 54; waves 53; *see also* digital media feminist activism
Fiske, J. 34
Ford, S. 30–31
Foucault, M., on power 48–50
Fourie, P. J. 47–48
freedom of expression 93, 109–111
friends 32–33, 72
Fuchs, C. 30, 93; *Social Media: A Critical Introduction* 24

Gajjala, A. 62–63
Geisler, G. 45, 52, 65–66
gender 55; equality 96, 109–110; norms 51; swapping 50; "talk" participants 103
gender-based violence (GBV) 1, 2, 44, 45, 47, 49, 56, 64–66, 74, 115; #MeToo campaign 76; enablers 100–101; examining through a feminist lens 6–7; as human rights issue 4; intimate partner violence (IPV) 2; "the manufacture of female fear" 18–22; patriarchy 20–22; in South Africa 2–7; South African statutes prohibiting 79–80; toxic masculinity 81; *see also* abuse; domestic violence; patriarchy
Geraghty, C. 40, 90
Giddens, A. 51
Gqola, D. P. 18, 22, 31
Graça Machel Trust 65
Graham, H. 105
Gray, J. 104
Green, J. 30–31

Habermas, J. 93
Hajru, A. 105
Hall, S. 48, 63
Haraway, D. 63
hashtags 75, 76; #BlackTwitter 99; *see also* #AmINext; #MeToo

Hawthorne, S. 61
Head, T. 98
Herbert, T. B. 15
Hill Collins, P. 44, 51; *Black Feminist Thought* 57; *Black Sexual Politics* 9, 45–46
Hobson, D. 38
home, violence against women at 4–5
hooks, b. 44, 45, 59, 99
human rights 4
humour 94–95

identity 45, 60, 66, 71, 72, 111; African 39, 55; Black 51; gender 50; online 46, 48–50; politics 93; "talk" participants 101, 102
Indigenous knowledge production 49, 59, 115
"inside"/"outside" discourse 71–73, 78–79, 100, 109–110
internet 37; women-centered online spaces 62–63; *see also* cyberfeminism
intersectionality 57
intimate partner violence (IPV) 2, 11, 12, 18, 31, 47, 77, 100–101; in *Scandal!* 13–16; stigma 17
Iqbal, N. 20
Izumi, K. 3

Jarret, H. 80
Jenkins, H. 30–31, 34, 103–104
Jezebel 9
Joachim, J. M. 92
Johnson, K. 12, 36
jokes 94–95

Kelly, L. 16–17
Kemp, S. 37
Khumalo, Z. 6
kkkk 94
Kozinets, R. V. 74
Kyung-Na, E. 31

labels 72–73
Laclau, E. 74

Lamia, M. C. 10
Langa, M. 8
language 49, 94, 116–117; slang 108; of "talk" 107–108; use of the term "feminism" 59
Lee, S. 6
Levenson, M., *The Spectacle of Intimacy* 11
Levine, E. 106
Löwstedt, A. 18; on femicide 19

Mahlaba, G. 6, 8, 9, 101
Malawi 82
Mammy 9
Mann, K. L. 60, 87
"manosphere" 19–20, 81
"manufacture of female fear" 18–22
marriage 49, 64, 91, 95–98, 110; and property rights 98
masculinity 51, 52, 60, 92; toxic 81
matriarchal system 55
Maynard, M. 62
McLaurin, I. 43
McQuail, D. 25
meaning 63, 72, 87
media 1, 32; audience 34–35; new 48, 60, 64, 87; representation 47–48
Mekgwe, P. 50, 57
memes 94–95
#MenAreTrash 5
Meta *see* Facebook
meta text 34
#MeToo 76, 99
Millennials 96–97
Mills, S. 116
misogyny 59, 95
mobile devices 36–37
Mokoena, K. 6
Montreal Massacre 8
Morgan, R. 58
Moruakgomo, P. 9, 109
Mosese, T. 90
Mouffe, C. 74
Mrwetyana, U. 2, 6, 75
Mthembu, N. 100

name-calling 86
Namibia 82
Nelson, O. 49–50
netnography 22, 23, 74
network society 32
new media 60, 64, 87; online identity 48
Nhlapo, J. 6
non-governmental organisations, Graça Machel Trust 65
norms: gender 51; social media conversation 108
Ntuli, P. 60
nxa 94

online identity 46, 48–50, 103
Oyewumi, O. 44–45, 52–53, 55, 58, 99

Paltoglou, G. 34
Pateman, C. 98
patriarchal violence 12–13
patriarchy 44, 51, 91, 92, 97; African 51–53; gender-based violence (GBV) and 20–22; in South Africa 21
Phiri, M. 88
physical abuse 2; psychological damage 3
Pilcher, J. 50
Pillay, A. 4, 5
Pistorius, O. 5–6
Pizzey, E., *Scream Quietly or the Neighbors Will Hear* 17
politics 74; of difference 55; identity 93
Porter, D. 88
postmodern feminism 46, 96; Gens on 63–64
post-traumatic stress disorder (PTSD) 17
power 58, 61, 62, 64, 91; Foucault on 48–50; patriarchal 21
praxis 59
prime time television 36
property rights 98
protest 76–77
psychological abuse 13
public sphere 93, 94
public/private dichotomy 97

qualitative methods 73

racism 57
Radford, J. 16–17
rape 22, 80
Renate, K. 61
reporting violence against women 5
representation 40, 46–47, 53, 74, 88, 91, 106–107; gender 51; and power 48–50; self- 48
reproductive rights 4
reverse discrimination 101
Richardson, D. 91
rights 45; freedom of expression 93, 109–111; property 98; reproductive 4; women's 3, 53, 100; *see also* human rights
Robinson, V. 91
Ross, S. M. 35

Sapphire 9
Saunders, L. 80
Sayyid, B. 72–73, 116
Scandal! 1–3, 5, 6, 31, 37, 39, 43, 49, 51, 64, 77–78, 81; common couple violence 12–13; Facebook fans 33, 34; Facebook page 38–40; Gloria Rangaka 8–9; Obakeng Rangaka 9–18; representation 47–48; teasers 101
second wave feminism 53, 56
Segal, M. T. 94–95
Seiter, C. 77
Serebrenik, A. 49–50
Shona 102
signification 73, 74
single divorced women, stigma 88
slacktivism 79–80
slang 108
slavery 22
smartphones 36–37
Smith, A. 105
soap opera/s 2, 7, 25, 37, 88, 90, 91, 109; Facebook fan pages 35; fandom 103–104; producers 106; representation 47–48; storytelling 38–39; "talk" 39
"social" 32
social justice 43

social media 2, 3, 7, 21, 30, 106, 108, 115, 117; #AmINext 1; audience 34–35; Black feminism 56–57; campaigns 8, 66, 98–99; fandom 35; fans 32; friends 32–33; "inside"/"outside" discourse 71–73; "Like" button 23–24; "manosphere" 19–20; meta text 34; name-calling 86; neologisms 94; online identity 48; representation 47–48; "talk" 22–25, 31; trolling 86; *see also* #AmINext
social television 31, 36–37; audience 34–35; fandom 35
socialisation 110
sociality 30, 31
solidarity 58
Soros, G. 31
South Africa/n 44; Apartheid 57–58, 97–98; domestic violence 65; Facebook 25; femicide 5–6, 18; Femicide National Strategic Plan Steering Committee 1; feminism 53, 54; gender-based violence (GBV) 2–7; National Conference on Violence against Women 4; patriarchal system 21; slang 108; soap operas 37–39; social media 31; statutes prohibiting violence against women 79–80; violence against women campaigns 8; Women's Month 8
South African Society of Obstetricians and Gynaecology 77
Spelman, E. 55–56
Spence, L. 2, 111
Spender, D. 116–117
"spreadable media" 31
Steady, F. C. 58, 60
Steenkamp, R. 5–6
stereotypes 86–87; Black women 9
stigma 17; of single divorced women 87–88
Stone, A. R. 50
storytelling, through soap operas 38–39
Sundén, J. 49
symbolic realm 63

Tadia, N. 45
"talk" 1, 10, 13, 22–25, 30–31, 40, 44, 53, 59, 64, 85, 99; about gender violence 3; awareness of domestic abuse 88–89; awareness of Gloria's role as a victim 89–90; awareness of Obakeng as an abuser 86; disgust 94; Facebook fan pages 33; and freedom of expression 109–111; gendered 93; humour 94; "inside"/"outside" discourse 71–73; lexicon 107–108; meta text 34; participants 101, 102; as signifying practice 73; soap operas 38–39; social depth 73; textual 49; *see also* gender-based violence (GBV); social media
technology 61
television 7, 23, 88; fandom 35; prime time 36; representation 47–48, 91, 92; social 31, 34–37
textual "talk" 49
Thompson, L. J. 15
Tifft, L. R. 20
toxic masculinity 81
trolling 86
Turkle, S. 50
Tweyi, A. 6
Twitter 25, 76; #AmINext 1, 2, 6, 18, 34–35, 38, 47, 48, 56–57; #CountMeIn 8; #MenAreTrash 5; "Like" button 23–24; *see also* social media

Ubuntu feminism 54
UN Declaration on the Elimination of Violence against Women 2–4
UN International Day for the Elimination of Violence against Women 7
Universal Declaration of Human Rights: Article 3 6; Article 5 6

van Hemert, I. 109
Vasilescu, B. 49–50
Victims of Crime Survey 2016/17 100
violence 7; common couple 12–13; family 22; intimate partner 2, 11,

12; patriarchal 12–13; patriarchy 20–22; against poor women 11; systemic 52, 65, 92; toxic masculinity 81; Wiseman on 19–20
violence against women 80, 116; campaigns 98–99; enablers 100–101; at home 4–5; "the manufacture of female fear" 18–22; rape 22; reporting 5; in *Scandal!* 13–16; socio-economic factors 20; in South Africa 2–7; *see also* gender-based violence (GBV)
Violence against women in South Africa: A Country in Crisis 92

Walby, S. 52, 97
"What's on your mind?" 32
Whelehan, I. 50
Willis, C. E. 5, 21
Wiseman, E., on violence against women 19–20
Wohn, D. Y. 31
Wolmark, J. 61
women: -centered online spaces 62–63; "of colour" 45–46; property rights 98; representation 40; rights 3, 53; systemic oppression 52; *see also* gender
World AIDS Day 7–8
World Economic Forum (WEF) 31
Wright, E. M. 12–13
Wu, K. 81

Yoruba 52, 55

Zac, L. 72–73, 116
Zibi, S., *Raising the Bar: Hope and Renewal in South Africa* 80
Zizek, S. 6
Zuckerberg, M. 31, 104